A NEW APPROACH
to EAR TRAINING

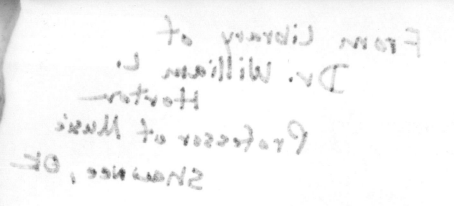
Another Norton Programed Text in Music Theory

Scales, Intervals, Keys and Triads
John Clough

Also by Leo Kraft
(with Sol Berkowitz and Gabriel Fontrier)

A New Approach to Sight Singing

NORTON PROGRAMED TEXTS
IN MUSIC THEORY

A NEW APPROACH
to EAR TRAINING

A PROGRAMED COURSE IN
MELODIC DICTATION

by LEO KRAFT

Queens College of the
City University of New York

W·W·NORTON & COMPANY·INC· *New York*

Library of Congress Catalog Card No. 67-15817

Printed in the United States of America

2 3 4 5 6 7 8 9 0

INTRODUCTION

The purpose of this program is to teach you to recognize and write down tonal melodies. Everyone can hear melodies and enjoy them. But the musician must know what he is hearing. He must identify the notes he is hearing and the scale that they belong to, he must grasp the structure of the rhythm, and he must hear and retain the melody as a whole.

Learning to hear is part of the professional training of every music student. For a serious musician, training and improving his ear is a lifetime preoccupation. The first part of that training can be accomplished by means of this program. Thanks to the self-teaching method known as programed instruction, you may take an individual course in elementary ear training.

A college course is usually built on a basic theoretical concept. The underlying principle behind this program is that of tonality. All of the music studied in this course, and in most of your music courses, is tonal. Put simply, this means that in any given piece all of the notes are related to the tonic. In your theory courses, you learn how the notes are related to the tonic. In your ear-training course, you hear those relationships expressed in melody.

To help relate each note to the tonic, it is suggested that you use sol-fa syllables. After you hear each exercise, sing it back to yourself, using these syllables: in major, Do-Re-Mi-Fa-Sol-La-Ti-Do; in the melodic minor, used in this course, ascending: Do-Re-Me (pronounced May)-Fa-Sol-La-Ti-Do, descending: Do-Te (Tay)-Le (Lay)-Sol-Fa-Me-Re-Do. What is the advantage of using syllables? They embody the relationships that operate in the major and minor scales—that is, they express melodic function. When you think or sing "Sol," you are saying "fifth degree of the scale" in one syllable, and thus you specify its relationship to Do, the first degree of the scale. Each sol-fa syllable expresses a particular relationship to the tonic, and any two syllables, of course, spell out a melodic interval. Thus you will learn melodic intervals, but in a tonal context rather than mechanically. Thinking in syllables also helps you to remember the melodic patterns that recur frequently in tonal music, such as Do-Mi-Sol. Use of the sol-fa

syllables is not the only way to think of tonal melodies, and if your instructor so chooses, another method may be employed.

Since the musician's goal is to hear the melody as a whole rather than to hear one or a few notes at a time, the program teaches patterns of melody. The course also stresses melodic shape and contour, teaching the perception of melody in whole phrases. These aims are partly served by the questions and cues that precede some of the exercises. Often the answers to the questions will be in the form of noteheads—that is, simply the head of a note—which you jot down quickly in the appropriate place on the worksheet. These answers, in turn, are incorporated in your final answer.

So far we have discussed pitch; what about rhythm? Rhythmic perception is taught by starting with the simplest rhythms and proceeding step by step to the more complex. As each new aspect of rhythm is introduced, it is identified and frequently illustrated. But the development of rhythmic perception depends to some extent upon your ability to beat time consistently as you sing back the melodies.

Since the rhythms of the opening Lessons are quite simple, beating time should be started at the outset of the course. Using the standard conducting gestures, which are illustrated on the page titled "How to Study Unit One," you may try to beat time even while you are hearing the melody, but be sure to beat time while you are singing the tune. The more you practice this skill, the less you will have to think about it. By beating time consistently, you can learn to keep your bearings within the measure, even if you can't identify all of the rhythms on first hearing.

Just as you have to practice a musical instrument regularly in order to develop your skill and confidence, so you have to practice ear training regularly if you want to develop skills of aural perception. Listening skill can be acquired over a period of time by most students. It cannot be picked up quickly by doing several Lessons in rapid succession. There is no way to cram. Plan your work so that you can listen regularly, and keep track of your progress by checking off the Lessons on the Student Record Sheet that is included with each Unit.

ORGANIZATION OF THE COURSE

This course consists of four units. Each Unit contains 7 basic Lessons (identified with single letters, A through G), 7 supplementary Lessons (identified with double letters, AA through GG), a Practice Lesson, a Review, and a Test. At several points in the course, there are additional Lessons (identified with triple letters), giving drill in special topics.

If you score at least 90% in both pitch and rhythm on the basic single-letter Lesson, you proceed to the next single-letter Lesson; if you score less, you proceed to the corresponding double-letter Lesson, for additional practice at the same level before going on. Specific instructions are given on each worksheet.

The Practice Lesson, following Lessons G and GG in each Unit, is optional. It serves as additional material for students who wish to prepare for the Test by working on melodies more difficult than those on the Test.

The Review and Test are given in class by the instructor; they are not included on the tape recordings.

GENERAL PROCEDURE

To start a Lesson, you need:

1) this workbook, which includes instructions, your worksheets, and the answers;

2) tape playback equipment, which may be operated either by you or from a control station;

3) the tape for the Lesson to be studied (you do not need to have the tape yourself if it will be played from a control station).

If you are operating the playback yourself, familiarize yourself with the operation of the tape machine before you go any further. Adjust the earphones so that you feel comfortable. Be sure you have ample flat surface on which to write. Use pencil, and have an extra one available.

Specific instructions are given at the beginning of each Unit, because the format of the Lessons varies in some details from one Unit to the next. However, the following basic procedure is followed in all lessons.

When the playback starts, you will hear the Lesson identified. This is often followed by introductory material, which is printed on the worksheet and spoken on the tape; when you see three dots (. . .) on your worksheet, a musical illustration is heard at the corresponding place on the tape. Follow this introductory material closely.

Then you will hear the identification of the first exercise: "Number One," followed by the sound of the tonic note of the first melody's key. (In Unit One, this note is also the same as the first note of each melody and is printed on your worksheet in the appropriate place, in correct rhythmic value.) Besides indicating the tonic, this note also serves as a signal that the first playing of the melody is about to begin.

Listen to the first playing of the melody, then sing back the entire melody (using sol-fa syllables or an alternative method), beating time as you sing. Write down as much of the melody as you can remember. Singing the melody back fixes it in your mind and makes it easier to write out. If you only remember the beginning, or the end, or a phrase from the middle, write it down as best you can in the 30 seconds provided.

At the end of the 30 seconds, you will hear the preliminary note again, followed by a second playing of the entire melody. Use this second playing to complete your answer and check it. (In later Lessons, the melody will be played a third time.)

At the end of another 45 seconds, you will hear the announcement identifying the next exercise. Follow the same procedure for each exercise.

(NOTE: On the single-letter Lessons of Units One and Two, there is a rapid-advance feature: If you make no errors in the first five exercises, you have completed the Lesson, and you may proceed to the next single-letter Lesson. After the fifth exercise of these Lessons, you will hear "Check One through Five now." Tear your worksheet, from the bottom up, along the perforation, until you reach the dotted line on the back; fold along this dotted line so that you can see the correct answers to Exercises 1 through 5. Check your answers for any errors; one minute will be allowed for checking. If there are no errors, you have completed the Lesson; make a check mark in the circle after Exercise 5, mark your Student Record Sheet according to the instruction, sign the worksheet, tear it out, and turn it in. If you find any errors, unfold the page to its normal position, and proceed with Exercise 6, which follows after the one minute allowed for checking.)

After the final exercise is heard for the last time and the time allotted for writing has elapsed, you will hear "Score your answers now." For the correct answers to exercises in the upper part of the page, follow the procedure described above for checking the answers to Exercises 1-5 in Units One and Two: tear the worksheet from the bottom up, along the perforation, until you reach the dotted line on the back, and fold along that line. The answers to exercises in the lower part of the page are found by tearing the worksheet down from the top and folding along the dashed line. Score your exercises according to the detailed instructions given on page 6, find your next instruction on the reverse of the worksheet, and mark your Student Record Sheet accordingly. Sign your worksheet, tear it out, and turn it in.

(NOTE: In Units Three and Four, the single-letter Lessons are in two parts, the first of which consists of exercises giving you special practice in various aspects of ear training. In these Lessons, Part 1 is not scored. Part 2 is similar to the Lessons of the first two Units.)

SCORING

When you have folded your worksheet according to the appropriate instructions, so that you can see both your answers and the correct answers, you are ready to score. First score your answer to the first exercise for pitch: mark an x *over* any incorrect pitch, or any pitch you have added or omitted. Then score the same exercise for rhythm: mark an x *under* any beat that is not correctly notated, or that is omitted. Follow the same procedure for each exercise. The following examples illustrate how this method works.

A.   All pitches are correct. The last beat in bar 1 does not have the correct rhythmic notation. Although two notes are written on the incorrect fourth beat, only one is marked because only one beat is involved. In bar 2, both first and second beats are incorrect even though only one note is misplaced, and two x's are marked.

B.   In bar 1, two pitches are incorrect. In bar three, the sharps required to spell La-Ti in this minor key are omitted, counting as two errors. The rhythm is correct.

C. Five pitches are incorrect, and there is an extra one, making a total of six x's. In bar 1, the rhythm of both first and second beats is notated incorrectly, and the same is true of bar 2. The duration of the last note of the melody is not correct. The last note of any melody should be marked with only one x for a rhythm error, no matter how many beats are concerned. Do not score rests until Unit Four.

When you have completed marking all the exercises, you are ready to determine your score. Count up the total number of pitch x's, and write it in the space marked: (Px). Count up the total number of rhythm x's, and write it in the space marked: (Rx). Subtract your Px and Rx from the given figures to get your P-score and R-score. These are the figures you compare with the instructions on the reverse of the worksheet, to see which Lesson you should do next.

What is the basis for the scoring? The figures given represent the total number of pitches and beats in a Lesson. You are required to write 90% or more of both pitches and rhythms correctly before proceeding to the next level of difficulty; if you do not achieve 90%, the instruction on the reverse of the worksheet directs you to another Lesson on the same level, for further drill.

*　*　*

Remember that this program is a course of study, not a test. The purpose of scoring is to regulate your progress, to indicate the need for additional work, and to pinpoint your difficulties. The purpose of turning in your worksheets is to give your instructor an opportunity to diagnose your work. Your scores in the Lessons do not determine your grades. Your grades are determined by the Tests, which conclude each Unit and are given in class. The program prepares you for these Tests and, beyond that, for music listening both in the classroom and outside of it.

UNIT ONE

I I I I I I I I I I I I I I I I I I I

STUDENT RECORD SHEET

Circle the Lesson you are to do next.

After completing that Lesson, draw a line through the circle, and circle the Lesson the instructions tell you to do next.

Keep this sheet up to date. It is intended solely for your guidance.

Ⓐ   AA

B   BB

C   CC

D   DD

E   EE

F   FF

G   GG

Starting date _____

Completion date _____

HOW TO STUDY UNIT ONE

Before starting Unit One, be sure you have read carefully the sections on "General Procedure" and "Scoring" (pp. 6-7).

Single-Letter Lessons

a. Follow on your worksheet the introductory material, while it is spoken on the tape. The three dots (. . .) on the worksheet indicate a musical illustration on the tape.

b. After the announcement of the exercise number, the preliminary note (the tonic) is heard; in Unit One, this is the same as the first note of the melody, and is given on the worksheet, in correct rhythmic value.

c. The melody is played, followed by a 30-second pause. During this pause, sing back the tune, beating time as you sing, and write down as much of the melody as you can.

d. The melody is heard again, preceded by the preliminary note and followed by a 45-second pause. Use this hearing to complete and check your answer.

e. The same procedure (steps b-d) is followed for each exercise.

f. After Exercise 5, you will hear "Now check One through Five." You will have one minute to do this. For the correct answers, tear the worksheet UP from the bottom along the perforation and fold along the dotted line. If you have made no errors, you have completed the Lesson. Make a check mark in the circle and read the instruction following Exercise 5. Mark your Student Record Sheet accordingly, sign the worksheet, remove it, and hand it in. If you have made any errors, proceed to the next step. (Do not score at this point.)

g. Do Exercises 6-8 following the procedure in steps b-d above.

h. After Exercise 8, mark your answers. For correct answers to Exercises 1-5, again fold the worksheet UP from the bottom along the dotted line. When you have marked 1-5, find the correct answers to 6-8 by tearing DOWN from the top and folding along the dashed line. Mark and score your answers according to the following instructions.

Scoring (for full details, see p. 6).

- Mark x *over* any incorrect pitch.
- Mark x *under* any incorrect beat. (Do not score rests.)
- Add up the number of pitch x's (*over* the notes) in the Lesson and enter in the space marked: (Px).
- Add up the number of rhythm x's (*under* the notes) in the Lesson and enter in the space marked: (Rx).
- Subtract from the given figures to obtain your pitch score (P-score) and your rhythm score (R-score).

i. Turn the worksheet over to find the next instruction. Mark your Student Record Sheet accordingly, sign the worksheet, remove it, and hand it in.

Double-Letter Lessons

Follow the procedure above, omitting Steps a and f.

NOTE: If there are any Lessons that you do not have to do, tear them out so that this instruction page will always conveniently face the worksheet you are using.

Basic Conducting Patterns

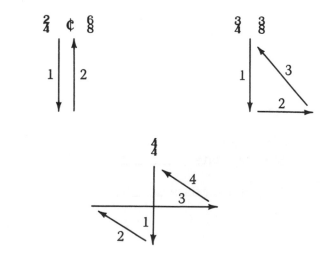

Name:

Date: Instructor:

We start with an illustration of a melody fragment using only the first three notes of the major scale: Do, Re, Mi. The melody starts on Do. Which note is the highest? . . . You heard that Mi was the highest. Now we add Fa and Sol. Which is the high point? . . . This time, Sol was the highest, and the melody again began and ended with Do. Adding La and Ti, we hear all of the notes of the major scale, not necessarily in order . . . The high point was La, and you heard Ti just below Do. Now proceed to Exercise 1.

③ Did you hear the high point in 2? Listen for the low point in 3, and jot it down.

④ The last note of the melody does not continue to the last bar line, as indicated.

⑤ Be sure to indicate the high point.

IF NO MISTAKES TO THIS POINT, PROCEED TO LESSON B.

⑦ Indicate both high and low points.

Scoring: 74   83

          -        (Px)   -   (Rx)

_____ (P-score)   _____ (R-score)   NEXT INSTRUCTION ON REVERSE

- -

If P-score is 67 or more
AND R-score is 75 or more,
proceed to Lesson B;
otherwise, proceed to AA.

. . . .

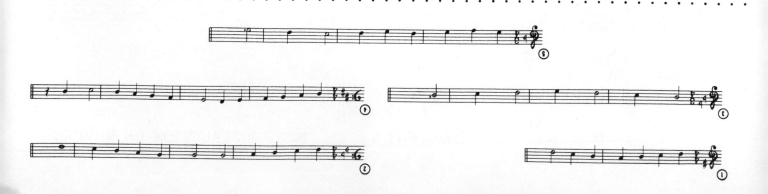

Name:

Date: Instructor:

① Indicate the high point.

② Listen for the low point.

③ Find both the high and low points.

④

⑤

⑥

⑦

⑧

Scoring: 72   84

        -      (Px)   -   (Rx)

_____ (P-score)   _____ (R-score)   NEXT INSTRUCTION ON REVERSE

If P-score is 65 or more
AND R-score is 76 or more,
proceed to Lesson B;
otherwise, repeat Lesson A.

Name:

Date: Instructor:

Lesson B includes melodies in the minor mode. You can tell from the given note whether an exercise is in the major or the minor mode. In this program, the following minor scale is used: ascending Do-Re-Me (pronounced May)-Fa-Sol-La-Ti-Do; descending Do-Te (Tay)-Le (Lay)-Sol-Fa-Me-Re-Do. Listen again to the difference between the rising . . . and falling forms. . . . Now proceed to Exercise 1.

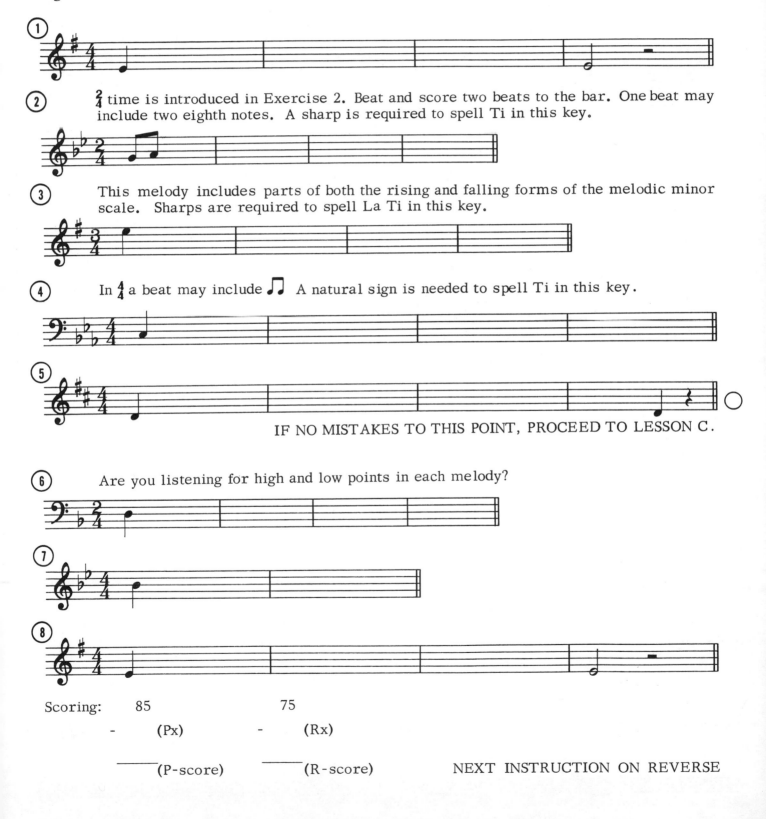

② ²⁄₄ time is introduced in Exercise 2. Beat and score two beats to the bar. One beat may include two eighth notes. A sharp is required to spell Ti in this key.

③ This melody includes parts of both the rising and falling forms of the melodic minor scale. Sharps are required to spell La Ti in this key.

④ In ⁴⁄₄ a beat may include ♫ A natural sign is needed to spell Ti in this key.

IF NO MISTAKES TO THIS POINT, PROCEED TO LESSON C.

⑥ Are you listening for high and low points in each melody?

Scoring: 85   75

          -      (Px)   -   (Rx)

_____ (P-score)   _____ (R-score)   NEXT INSTRUCTION ON REVERSE

If P-score is 76 or more
AND R-score is 67 or more,
proceed to Lesson C;
otherwise, proceed to BB.

Name:

Date: Instructor:

① Listen to the difference between Le, which has a "down" tendency, and La, which has an "up" tendency.

② Major or minor?

③

④ Compare the falling and rising forms of the minor scale.

⑤

⑥

⑦

⑧

Scoring: 72   73

        -      (Px)   -   (Rx)

        _____ (P-score)   _____ (R-score)   NEXT INSTRUCTION ON REVERSE

If P-score is 65 or more
AND R-score is 66 or more,
proceed to Lesson C;
otherwise, repeat Lesson B.

Name:

Date: Instructor:

The basic materials of melody are scales and chord patterns. The melodies of Lessons A and B were built on scale patterns only. Lesson C introduces chord patterns. All of the melodies in this Lesson are based on the tonic triad. Some are built on the major triad . . . ., some on the minor triad. . . .

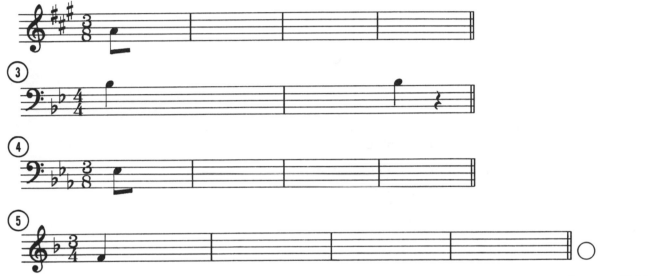

② ⅜ time is introduced here. The dotted quarter note represents one beat. Beat and score one to the bar. One beat may include

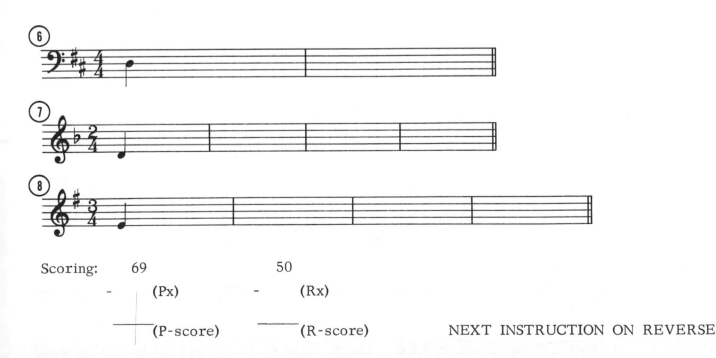

IF NO MISTAKES TO THIS POINT, PROCEED TO LESSON D.

Scoring: 69   50

‐   (Px)   ‐   (Rx)

——— (P-score)   ——— (R-score)   NEXT INSTRUCTION ON REVERSE

If P-score is 62 or more
AND R-score is 45 or more,
proceed to Lesson D;
otherwise, proceed to CC.

Name:

Date: Instructor:

① As you sing back each melody, be sure to beat time.

Scoring: 63   50

        ‒   (Px)   ‒   (Rx)

        _____(P-score)   _____(R-score)   NEXT INSTRUCTION ON REVERSE

If P-score is 57 or more
AND R-score is 45 or more,
proceed to Lesson D;
otherwise, repeat Lesson C.

Name:

Date: Instructor:

In Lesson D, both scale and chord patterns are used. Many times, a scale motion may be thought of as filling the space between the notes of a chordal skip. The notes which fill the space are called passing tones (PT). The skip Do-Mi . . . may be filled in with Re . . . . The skip Mi-Sol . . . may be filled in or elaborated with Fa . . . . Two passing tones are used to cover the distance from Sol up to Do . . . . Another example shows an ascending triad followed by the notes of the descending scale . . . .

① Listen for the triad in bar 1, which is elaborated with passing tones in bar 2.

② From now on, when the melody ends without completing the bar, only the value of the final rest is given. Both a natural sign and a sharp are required to spell La Ti in this key.

③ In ₵ the half note is equal to one beat, both in conducting and scoring. Beat two to the bar. A beat may include ♩ or ♩♩

④

⑤ The rhythm ♩ ♫ in ¾ is introduced.

IF NO MISTAKES TO THIS POINT, PROCEED TO LESSON E.

⑥

⑦

⑧

Scoring: 72   57

            -      (Px)   -   (Rx)

_____ (P-score)   _____ (R-score)   NEXT INSTRUCTION ON REVERSE

If P-score is 65 or more
AND R-score is 51 or more,
proceed to Lesson E;
otherwise, proceed to DD.

Remember that the rhythm score for the last note of a melody is 1, no matter what
the duration of that note.

① Listen to the difference between the rising and falling forms of the minor mode.

② Remember to beat and score two to the measure in ¢.

③ Listen for the duration of the last note.

④ Memorize the last four notes and write them down quickly.

⑤

⑥

⑦ Jot down the high point.

⑧ To spell La Ti in this key, do you need sharps? flats? natural signs?

Scoring: 78   67

         -      (Px)   -   (Rx)

        _____ (P-score)   _____ (R-score)   NEXT INSTRUCTION ON REVERSE

If P-score is 70 or more
AND R-score is 60 or more,
proceed to Lesson E;
otherwise, repeat Lesson D.

Often you can recognize a contour or a pattern in a melody without being sure of all the notes. It is possible to write cues for yourself, which can be translated into actual notes on second hearing. If you hear . . ., you may recognize a scale passage without knowing all the notes, and you may recognize a familiar closing formula, Sol La Ti Do, and you might write cues:

Using these cues, complete on second hearing . . .   This technique can help you to hear longer melodies. The scale passage need not include the entire melody, but try to remember where it begins and ends.

You have a pause of 30 seconds to check your answer to this illustration. For the correct answer, tear the page up from the bottom and fold (do not score). Then turn to the next work-sheet and do Lesson E.

(Do not score.)

Name:

Date: Instructor:

① In ¢, a beat may include ♩♪♪♪

② Listen for the duration of the last note.

③ In ¢, a beat may include ♩ ♪♪

④

⑤ If a bar is repeated, write ——— over the repetition.

IF NO MISTAKES TO THIS POINT, PROCEED TO LESSON F.

⑥

⑦

⑧

Scoring: 100   76
                    -        (Px)   -   (Rx)

            ————(P-score)   ————(R-score)   NEXT INSTRUCTION ON REVERSE

If P-score is 90 or more
AND R-score is 69 or more,
proceed to Lesson F;
otherwise, proceed to EE.

① Scale and triad? Triad and scale?

②

③ Write down the last 4 notes after first hearing.

④ Can you locate the high point?

⑤

⑥

⑦

⑧

Scoring: 94   71

        -      (Px)   -   (Rx)

_____ (P-score)   _____ (R-score)   NEXT INSTRUCTION ON REVERSE

If P-score is 85 or more
AND R-score is 64 or more,
proceed to Lesson F;
otherwise, repeat Lesson E.

Name:

Date: Instructor:

In addition to passing tones, neighbor or auxiliary tones may be used to embellish a triad. The familiar Do Mi Sol . . . may be elaborated with upper neighbor tones (NT) . . . or, in another version, with lower NT. . . . A melody from a Beethoven sonata . . . is based on a triad, but the NT give it melodic substance.

① The opening of Brahms's Second Symphony is built on triads and NT.

② This exercise consists mostly of a triad and NT. Write down the first note in each bar as you listen the first time: then sing back, and complete the exercise.

③

④ Cue in scale passages as they are heard. The time signature **C** is equivalent to $\frac{4}{4}$.

⑤ Write down the first note in each bar as you listen, then sing back and try to complete the exercise.

IF NO MISTAKES TO THIS POINT, PROCEED TO LESSON G.

⑥

⑦ Your cues should include the high point of this melody.

⑧

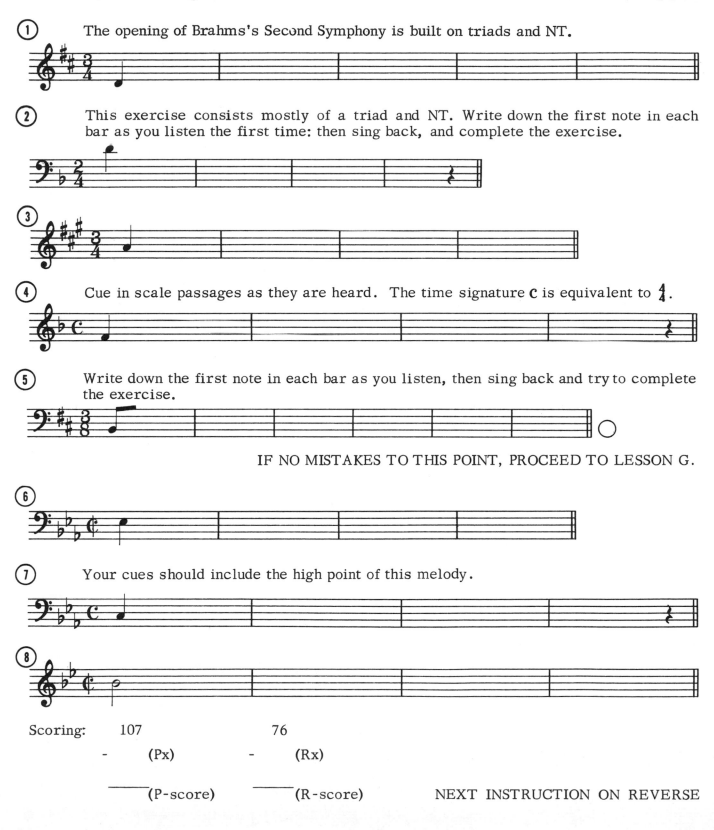

Scoring: 107   76

                  -      (Px)   -   (Rx)

_____ (P-score)   _____ (R-score)   NEXT INSTRUCTION ON REVERSE

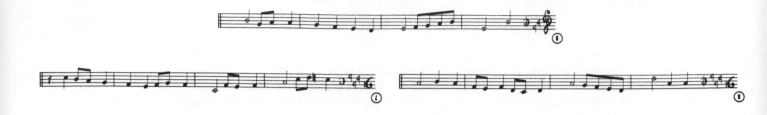

If P-score is 96 or more
AND R-score is 69 or more,
proceed to Lesson G;
otherwise proceed to FF.

Name:

Date: Instructor:

① Try to memorize the melody on one hearing by listening for the triad, which is embellished by NT.

②

③ Write your own cue for the scale passage.

④

⑤ Upper NT? Lower NT? Neither? Both?

⑥

⑦

⑧

Scoring: 95   76

          -      (Px)   -   (Rx)

_____(P-score)   _____(R-score)   NEXT INSTRUCTION ON REVERSE

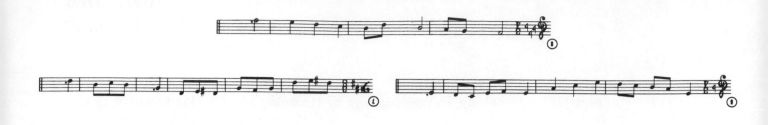

If P-score is 85 or more
AND R-score is 69 or more,
proceed to Lesson G;
otherwise, repeat Lesson F.

This is a summary Lesson. Techniques studied thus far are applied on a slightly more complex level. There are no cues.

IF NO MISTAKES TO THIS POINT, YOU HAVE COMPLETED UNIT ONE.
A PRACTICE LESSON IS AVAILABLE.

Scoring: 101   66

         -      (Px)   -   (Rx)

_____ (P-score)   _____ (R-score)   NEXT INSTRUCTION ON REVERSE

If P-score is 91 or more
AND R-score is 59 or more,
you have completed Unit One;
otherwise, proceed to GG.
A Practice Lesson is available after G or GG.

This is a summary Lesson. Techniques studied thus far are applied on a slightly more complex level. There are no cues. Remember to: jot down high and low points, make a note of scale passages, indicate triadic outlines whenever you can, listen for closing formulas.

Scoring: 94   60

- (Px)   - (Rx)

_____ (P-score)   _____ (R-score)   NEXT INSTRUCTION ON REVERSE

If P-score is 85 or more
AND R-score is 54 or more,
you have completed Unit One;
otherwise, repeat Lesson G.
A Practice Lesson is available after GG.

Name:

Date: Instructor:

The same procedure is followed as in the double-letter Lessons. Each melody, preceded by the preliminary note (tonic), is played twice.

Scoring: 177

    -        (total x)

    _____ (score)

CONVERSION TO LETTER GRADES ON REVERSE

Add pitch x's and rhythm x's to get
total number of errors (total x).

Conversion to letter grades:

A: 177-160

B: 159-142

C: 141-124

D: 123-106

Name:

Date: Instructor:

The same procedure is followed as in the double-letter Lessons, except that there are only five exercises. Each melody, preceded by the preliminary note (tonic), is played twice.

For the correct answers to Exercises 1-3, tear the worksheet UP from the bottom along the perforation, and fold along the dotted line. Find the correct answers to 4 and 5 by tearing DOWN from the top and folding along the dashed line. Add pitch x's and rhythm x's for total number of errors.

Scoring: 121

            -        (total x)

            _____ (score)   CONVERSION TO LETTER GRADES ON REVERSE

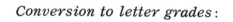

Conversion to letter grades:

    A: 121-110

    B: 109- 98

    C: 97- 86

    D: 85- 74

Name:

Date: Instructor:

The same procedure is followed as in the double-letter Lessons and the Review; there are only five exercises. Each melody, preceded by the preliminary note (tonic), is played twice.

Scoring: 109

          -     (total x)

          _____ (score)

UNIT TWO

II II II II II II II II II II II II II

STUDENT RECORD SHEET

Circle the Lesson you are to do next.

After completing that Lesson, draw a line through the circle, and circle the Lesson the instructions tell you to do next.

Keep this sheet up to date. It is intended solely for your guidance.

Ⓐ   AA   AAA

B   BB

C   CC

D   DD   DDD

E   EE

F   FF

G   GG

Starting date _____

Completion date _____

HOW TO STUDY UNIT TWO

Single-Letter Lessons

a. Follow on your worksheet the introductory material, while it is spoken on the tape. The three dots (. . .) on the worksheet indicate a musical illustration on the tape.

b. After the announcement of the exercise number, the preliminary note (the tonic) is heard; in Unit Two, this is the same as the first note of the melody, but it is no longer given on the worksheet. From the key signature, you can tell that the tonic may be either one of two possible pitches, depending on whether the melody is in the major or the minor mode. As you listen to the first playing, decide whether the melody is major or minor.

c. The melody is played, followed by a 30-second pause. During this pause, sing back the tune, beating time as you sing, and write down as much of the melody as you can. Starting with Lesson D in this Unit, bar lines are no longer given on the worksheet. Use the time signature as a cue to help locate the bar lines, and sketch them in quickly as you sing back the melody after the first hearing. Check your answer to be sure you have the same number of beats in each measure.

d. The melody is heard again, preceded by the preliminary note and followed by a 45-second pause. Use this hearing to complete and check your answer.

e. The same procedure (steps b-d) is followed for each exercise.

f. After Exercise 5, you will hear "Now check One through Five." You will have one minute to do this. For the correct answers, tear the worksheet UP from the bottom along the perforation and fold along the dotted line. If you have made no errors, you have completed the Lesson. Make a check mark in the circle and read the instruction following Exercise 5. Mark your Student Record Sheet accordingly, sign the worksheet, remove it, and hand it in. If you have made any errors, proceed to the next step. (Do not score at this point.)

g. Do Exercises 6 and 7 following the procedure in steps b-d above.

h. After Exercise 7, mark your answers. For correct answers to Exercises 1-5, again fold the worksheet UP from the bottom along the dotted line. When you have marked 1-5, find the correct answers to 6 and 7 by tearing DOWN from the top and folding along the dashed line.

Mark and score your answers according to the following instructions.

Scoring (for full details, see p. 6):

- Mark x *over* any incorrect pitch.
- Mark x *under* any incorrect beat. (Do not score rests.)
- If you select the wrong first note but write the melody correctly relative to that note, write 5 x's *over* the first note.
- Add up the number of pitch x's (*over* the notes) in the Lesson and enter in the space marked: (Px).
- Add up the number of rhythm x's (*under* the notes) in the Lesson and enter in the space marked: (Rx).
- Subtract from the given figures to obtain your pitch score (P-score) and rhythm score (R-score).

i. Turn the worksheet over to find the next instruction. Mark your Student Record Sheet accordingly, sign the worksheet, remove it, and hand it in.

Double-Letter Lessons

Follow the procedure above, omitting Steps a and f.

Triple-Letter Lessons

Follow the instructions given on the worksheets. Lesson AAA comprises additional drill in mode recognition, Lesson DDD in keeping count of the number of bars in a melody.

NOTE: If there are any Lessons that you do not have to do, tear them out so that this instruction page will always conveniently face the worksheet you are using.

Basic Conducting Patterns

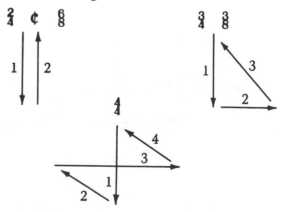

① Major or minor?

② In ⅜ time, beat and score two to the bar. ♩. is considered as the unit, one beat. A beat may include ♩. or ♫♪ or ♩♪ The rhythm of bar 1 is ♫♪ ♩.

We are already familiar with a NT, such as Mi-Fa-Mi . . . Now we hear an incomplete NT Fa-Mi . . . which may be preceded by a leap from Do . . . or from above . . . or from another note. Many Do-Fa skips can be heard as incomplete NT.

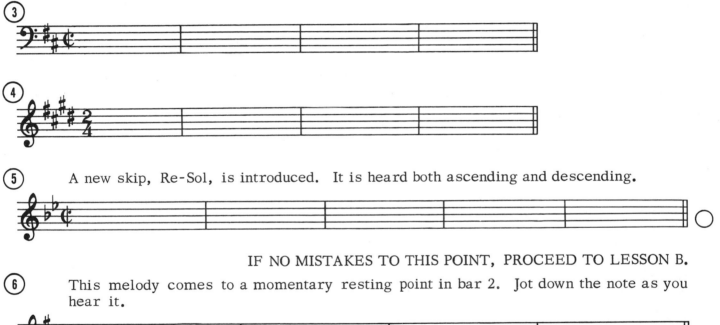

③

④

⑤ A new skip, Re-Sol, is introduced. It is heard both ascending and descending.

IF NO MISTAKES TO THIS POINT, PROCEED TO LESSON B.

⑥ This melody comes to a momentary resting point in bar 2. Jot down the note as you hear it.

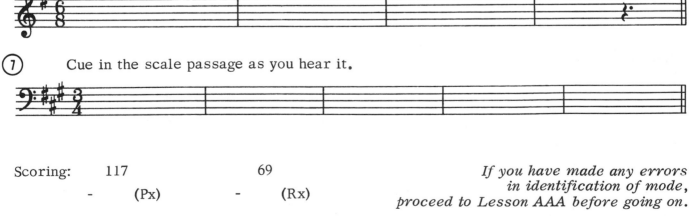

⑦ Cue in the scale passage as you hear it.

Scoring: 117   69

          -    (Px)   -   (Rx)

*If you have made any errors
in identification of mode,
proceed to Lesson AAA before going on.*

_____ (P-score)   _____ (R-score)

NEXT INSTRUCTION ON REVERSE

If P-score is 105 or more
AND R-score is 62 or more,
proceed to Lesson B;
otherwise, proceed to AA.

① Both Do-Fa and Re-Sol skips are included.

② Jot down the resting point (goal) in bar 2.

③

④

⑤ Write in the last bar first.

⑥

⑦

Scoring: 110   78

      -     (Px)   -   (Rx)

_____ (P-score)   _____ (R-score)

If you have made any errors
in identification of mode,
proceed to Lesson AAA before going on.

NEXT INSTRUCTION ON REVERSE

If P-score is 99 or more
AND R-score is 70 or more,
proceed to Lesson B;
otherwise, repeat Lesson A.

This Lesson consists of drills in distinguishing between major and minor modes.

PART 1.   You will hear ten melody fragments, each played once. For each, write "M" if the mode is major, "m" if minor. As soon as you hear the preliminary note, sing Do-Sol. Then listen for the third degree of the scale—is it Mi or Me?

1. _____   2. _____   3. _____   4. _____   5. _____

6. _____   7. _____   8. _____   9. _____   10. _____

Now you have 30 seconds to check and score. Tear this sheet up from the bottom and fold to see the answers to Part 1. Mark x over any answer that is not correct.

If all ten are correct, proceed to the Lesson previously indicated. If there are any errors, resume this Lesson.

PART 2.   The same procedure as in Part 1.

1. _____   2. _____   3. _____   4. _____   5. _____

6. _____   7. _____   8. _____   9. _____   10. _____

Tear this sheet down from the top and fold to see the answers to Part 2. Mark x over any incorrect answer. If all ten are correct, proceed to the Lesson previously indicated. If there are any errors, this Lesson should be repeated before you do Lesson D.

PART 1: 1. M   2. m   3. M   4. m   5. m

6. M   7. m   8. M   9. M   10. m

PART 2: 1. M   2. M   3. M   4. m   5. M

6. m   7. M   8. m   9. m   10. M

The lower NT . . . and the upper NT . . . may be combined . . . . This is often heard in an abbreviated form which omits the middle note, and is called the double NT (DN) . . . . Another form of the double NT (DN) . . . .

① This exercise is built on a triad, which is embellished with NT. As you listen, write down the first note in each bar.

② Rests which are required to fill the last bar are no longer cued in. Listen for the duration of the last note. Do not score rests. Continue to score the last note as 1, no matter what its duration.

When ♩ is one beat, as in ²⁄₄ or ³⁄₄ or ⁴⁄₄, a beat may include ♫♫ As an illustration, here is a theme from Beethoven's Second Symphony. A triad . . . is embellished with both PT and NT:

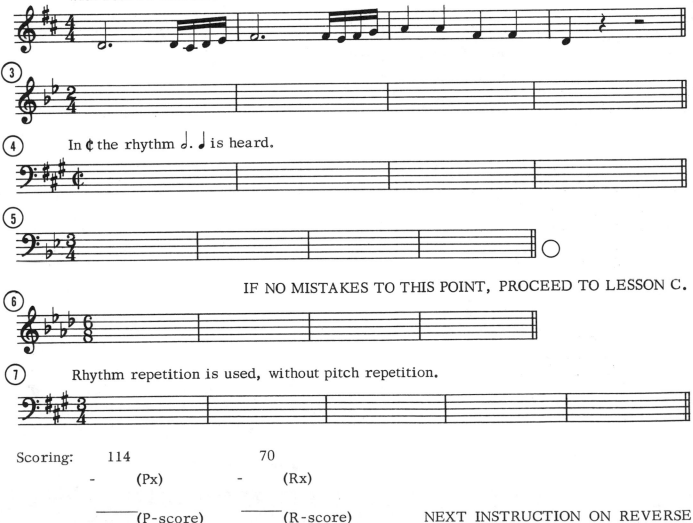

③

④ In ₵ the rhythm ♩. ♩ is heard.

⑤

IF NO MISTAKES TO THIS POINT, PROCEED TO LESSON C.

⑥

⑦ Rhythm repetition is used, without pitch repetition.

Scoring: 114   70

              -     (Px)   -   (Rx)

              _____ (P-score)   _____ (R-score)   NEXT INSTRUCTION ON REVERSE

If P-score is 103 or more
AND R-score is 63 or more,
proceed to Lesson C;
otherwise, proceed to BB.

Name:

Date: Instructor:

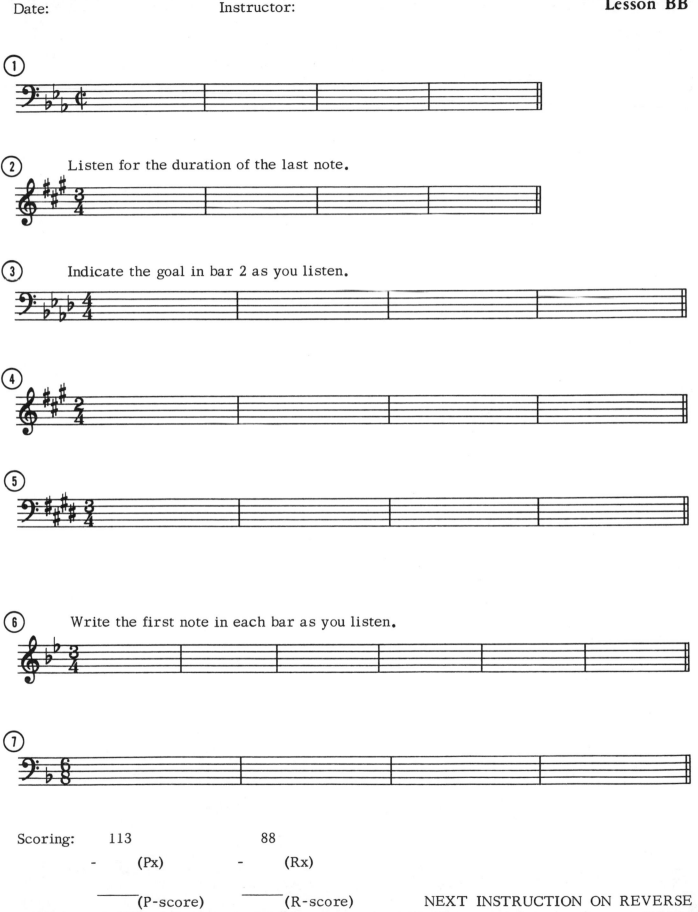

①

② Listen for the duration of the last note.

③ Indicate the goal in bar 2 as you listen.

④

⑤

⑥ Write the first note in each bar as you listen.

⑦

Scoring: 113   88

         -      (Px)   -   (Rx)

         _____ (P-score)   _____ (R-score)   NEXT INSTRUCTION ON REVERSE

If P-score is 102 or more
AND R-score is   77 or more,
proceed to Lesson C;
otherwise, repeat Lesson B.

(1) When the ♩ is the unit, a beat may include ♫♫

So far, chordal skips have been studied in the context of the tonic triad . . . . But we have also heard Re-Sol . . . and, as double NT, Ti-Re . . . . Now we take up the dominant triad, which may be heard as Sol-Ti-Re . . . in various combinations.

(2)

(3) Write down the goal in bar 2.

(4)

(5) This melody has quite a few notes. They may be heard as part of the tonic and dominant triads, with PT. Clue: identify the lowest note.

IF NO MISTAKES TO THIS POINT, PROCEED TO LESSON D.

(6)

(7) This melody centers on: Do? Mi? Sol?, embellished with DN.

Scoring: 127   83
              -        (Px)   -   (Rx)

_____ (P-score)   _____ (R-score)   NEXT INSTRUCTION ON REVERSE

If P-score is 114 or more
AND R-score is 75 or more,
proceed to Lesson D;
otherwise, proceed to CC.

①   Cue in the scale passage.

②   Listen for the duration of the last note.

③

④   Can you jot down the last 5 notes?

⑤

⑥   DN and PT embellish the triad.

⑦

Scoring: 127   71

         -     (Px)   -   (Rx)

         —— (P-score)   —— (R-score)   NEXT INSTRUCTION ON REVERSE

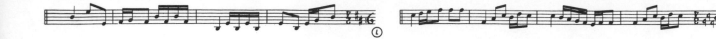

If P-score is 114 or more
AND R-score is 64 or more,
proceed to Lesson D;
otherwise, repeat Lesson C.

The rhythm ♩. ♪ is introduced with an illustration from Schubert's C major Symphony:

①

②

③ To the Sol-Ti-Re pattern studied in Lesson C we add Fa, giving Sol-Ti-Re-Fa, the dominant seventh chord.

④ The opening of Mozart's *Eine kleine Nachtmusik* is built on the tonic and dominant seventh chords. This excerpt does not end on Do.

⑤

IF NO MISTAKES TO THIS POINT, PROCEED TO LESSON E.

⑥ In ¢, ♩. ♩ is the equivalent of ♩. ♪ in ⅔ or ⁴⁄₄.

⑦

Scoring: 122   87

     -      (Px)   -   (Rx)

_____ (P-score)   _____ (R-score)

If you have made any errors
in writing bar lines,
proceed to Lesson DDD before going on.

NEXT INSTRUCTION ON REVERSE

If P-score is 110 or more
AND R-score is 78 or more,
proceed to Lesson E;
otherwise, proceed to DD.

① Distinguish between ♩♩♩ and ♩. ♪♩

②

③

④   Indicate repetition as you hear it.

⑤   Cue in the scale passage.

⑥

⑦

Scoring: 123   74

        -    (Px)   -   (Rx)

    _____ (P-score)   _____ (R-score)

If you have made any errors
in writing bar lines,
proceed to Lesson DDD before going on.

NEXT INSTRUCTION ON REVERSE

If P-score is 111 or more
AND R-score is 67 or more,
proceed to Lesson E;
otherwise, repeat Lesson D.

This Lesson affords practice in identifying the number of measures in a melody. The correct time signature for each melody is given. A preliminary note is sounded for each exercise, then the melody is played once. Beat time as you listen and count the number of measures you hear. Write only the number of measures, in the appropriate space below.

PART 1.   1. $\frac{4}{4}$ _____   2. $\frac{3}{4}$ _____   3. ¢ _____   4. $\frac{6}{8}$ _____   5. $\frac{4}{4}$ _____

6. $\frac{3}{4}$ _____   7. $\frac{2}{4}$ _____   8. C _____   9. ¢ _____   10. $\frac{3}{4}$ _____

Now you have 30 seconds to check and score. Tear this sheet up from the bottom and fold to see the answers to Part 1. Mark x over any answer that is not correct.

If all ten are correct, proceed to the Lesson previously indicated. If there are any errors, resume this Lesson.

PART 2.   1. ¢ _____   2. $\frac{2}{4}$ _____   3. $\frac{6}{8}$ _____   4. $\frac{4}{4}$ _____   5. $\frac{3}{4}$ _____

6. C _____   7. $\frac{3}{4}$ _____   8. $\frac{6}{8}$ _____   9. $\frac{3}{4}$ _____   10. C _____

Tear this sheet down from the top and fold to see the answers to Part 2. Mark x over any incorrect answer. Now proceed to the Lesson previously indicated.

PART 1: 1. 4   2. 5   3. 4   4. 4   5. 3
6. 5   7. 6   8. 4   9. 4   10. 5

PART 2: 1. 5   2. 4   3. 4   4. 4   5. 5
6. 8   7. 6   8. 5   9. 5   10. 4

Name:

Date: Instructor:

The melody pattern Do-La-Fa-Re is introduced in this Lesson . . . . In minor, it is Do-Le-Fa-Re . . . .

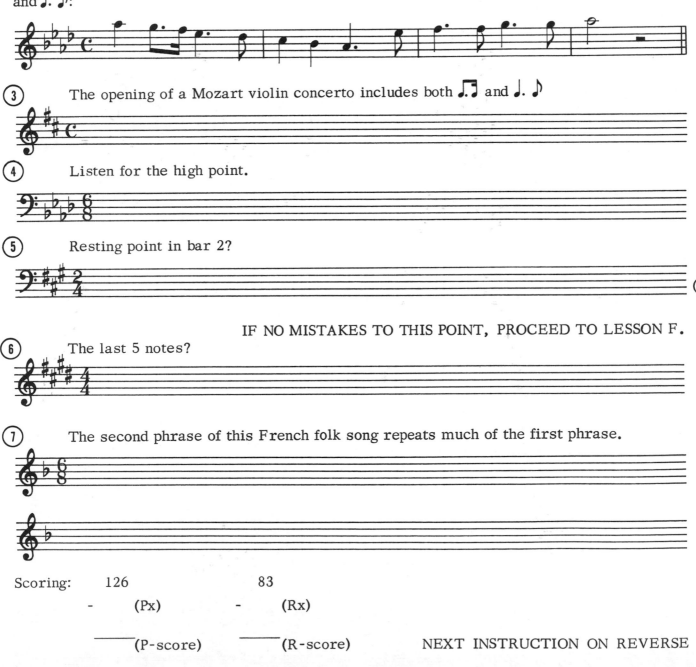

Scoring: 126   83

                -        (Px)   -   (Rx)

                _____(P-score)   _____(R-score)   NEXT INSTRUCTION ON REVERSE

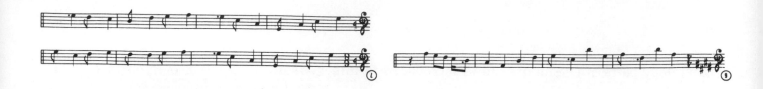

If P-score is 113 or more
AND R-score is 75 or more,
proceed to Lesson F;
otherwise, proceed to EE.

Name:

Date: Instructor:

①   (treble clef, one sharp, 3/4 — empty staff)

② Distinguish between ♩♩ and ♩. ♪

  (bass clef, two flats, 4/4 — empty staff)

③   (treble clef, one flat, 6/8 — empty staff)

④ Distinguish between ♩.♩ and ♩♩

  (bass clef, two sharps, 2/4 — empty staff)

⑤   (treble clef, four sharps, 3/4 — empty staff)

⑥ Remember that a beat in ¢ may include ♩. ♪, which is equivalent to ♩♩ in 2/4.

  (bass clef, one sharp, ¢ — empty staff)

⑦   (bass clef, two flats, C — empty staff)

Scoring: 110   75

          -    (Px)   -   (Rx)

     _____(P-score)   _____(R-score)   NEXT INSTRUCTION ON REVERSE

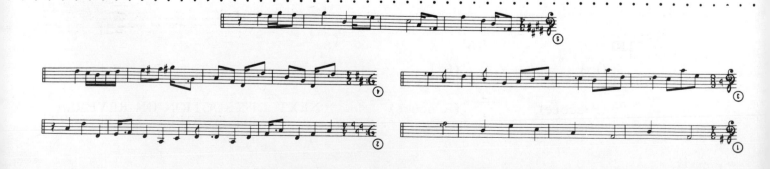

If P-score is 99 or more
AND R-score is 67 or more,
proceed to Lesson F;
otherwise, repeat Lesson E.

Name:

Date: Instructor:

We have studied Do-Fa skips . . . and the pattern Do-La-Fa-Re . . . Now listen to the tonic chord . . . followed by the subdominant, in the outline Do-Fa-La . . . . In minor . . . .

IF NO MISTAKES TO THIS POINT, PROCEED TO LESSON G.

Scoring: 148   85

　　　-   (Px)   -   (Rx)

_____(P-score)   _____(R-score)   NEXT INSTRUCTION ON REVERSE

If P-score is 133 or more
AND R-score is 76 or more,
proceed to Lesson G;
otherwise, proceed to FF.

Name:

Date: Instructor:

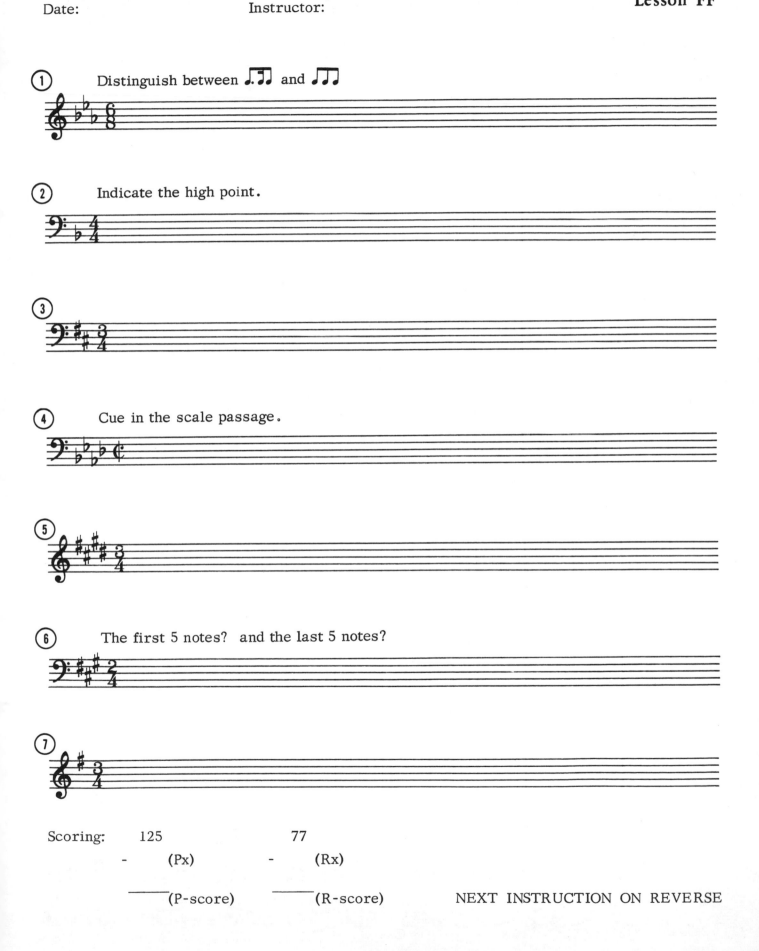

① Distinguish between ♩♫ and ♫♩

② Indicate the high point.

③

④ Cue in the scale passage.

⑤

⑥ The first 5 notes? and the last 5 notes?

⑦

Scoring: 125   77

        -      (Px)   -   (Rx)

        _____ (P-score)   _____ (R-score)   NEXT INSTRUCTION ON REVERSE

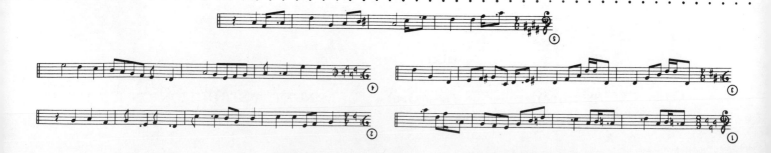

If P-score is 112 or more
AND R-score is 69 or more,
proceed to Lesson G;
otherwise, repeat Lesson F.

This is a summary Lesson. No new patterns of pitch or rhythm are introduced. There are no cues.

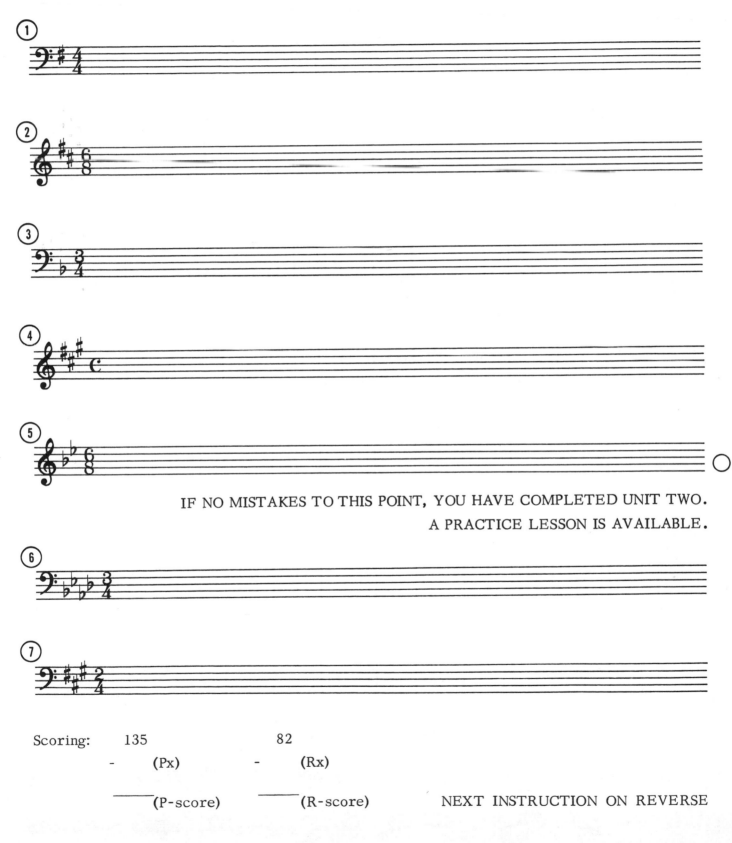

IF NO MISTAKES TO THIS POINT, YOU HAVE COMPLETED UNIT TWO.

A PRACTICE LESSON IS AVAILABLE.

Scoring: 135   82

    -      (Px)   -   (Rx)

_____ (P-score)   _____ (R-score)   NEXT INSTRUCTION ON REVERSE

If P-score is 121 or more
AND R-score is 74 or more,
you have completed Unit Two;
otherwise, proceed to GG.
A Practice Lesson is available after G or GG.

This is a summary Lesson. No new patterns of pitch or rhythm are introduced. There are no cues.

Scoring: 134   70

        -        (Px)   -   (Rx)

        _____(P-score)   _____(R-score)   NEXT INSTRUCTION ON REVERSE

If P-score is 121 or more
AND R-score is   63 or more,
you have completed Unit Two;
otherwise, repeat Lesson G.
A Practice Lesson is available after GG.

The same procedure is followed as in the double-letter Lessons. Each melody, preceded by the preliminary note (tonic), is played twice.

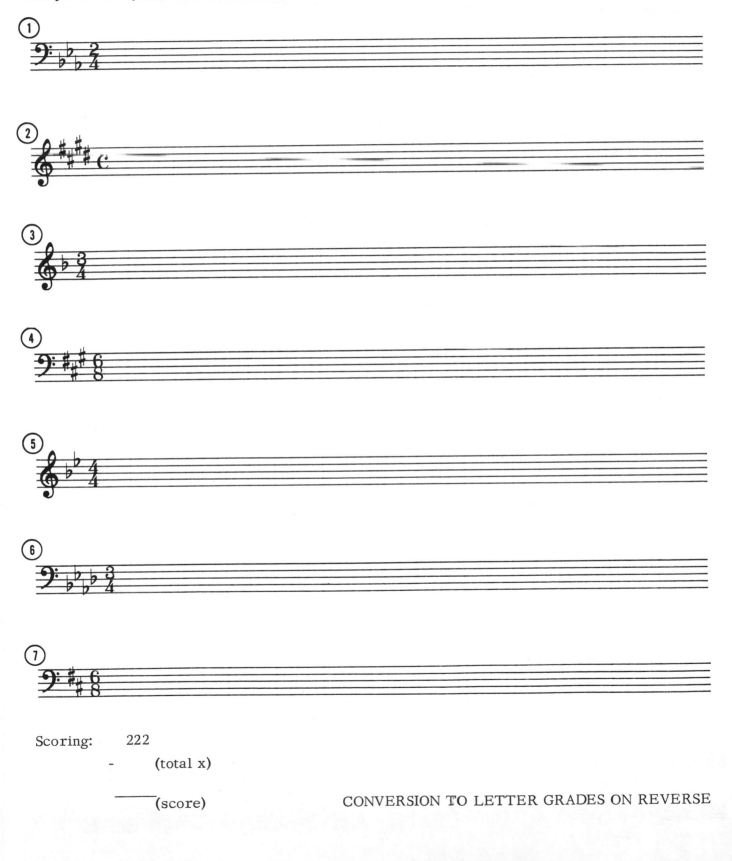

Scoring: 222

-          (total x)

_____ (score)

CONVERSION TO LETTER GRADES ON REVERSE

Conversion to letter grades:

    A: 222-201

    B: 200-179

    C: 178-153

    D: 153-131

NORTON PROGRAMED TEXTS
IN MUSIC THEORY

INSTRUCTOR'S MANUAL for

A NEW APPROACH
to EAR TRAINING

A SELF-INSTRUCTION PROGRAM

by **LEO KRAFT**

Queens College of the
City University of New York

W·W·NORTON & COMPANY·INC· *New York*

ABOUT THIS COURSE

What is the purpose of this course?

The purpose of this course is to develop the ability to hear and write down tonal melodies. Such ability is generally regarded as one of the professional skills of a musician. The teaching of ear training at American colleges encounters many obstacles; it is very time-consuming, there is little agreement on a conceptual basis for the course, there does not exist a progressively graded body of material for study, many students come to college with little foundation in musicianship, and they bring a wide diversity of educational backgrounds. *A New Approach to Ear Training* represents a systematic attempt to cope with these obstacles.

The author developed this course to meet the needs of his students in the freshman theory classes at Queens College. The program was given concurrently with beginning courses in harmony and sight singing. The only prerequisites for this program are the ability to read music (including both treble and bass clefs) and a knowledge of scales and keys.

As in all programed instruction, the student has the enormous advantage of what amounts to individual teaching, which he absorbs at his own speed. The course is composed in such a way that the faster student may cover the ground quite rapidly, without skipping any of the content, while the student who needs more drill at any stage of his study will find it. The time to be allotted for the course is best determined by the instructor, who can choose from several alternate possibilities.

Since all of the melodies in the course are tonal, the principles and operations of traditional tonality underlie the program. Recognition of the relationship of all notes to the tonic (tonal function), of scale patterns, of chordal outlines, identification of embellishing tones and of notes that may be considered as outlining the structure of a melody—all these are stressed repeatedly. But while the principles of tonality form the conceptual basis of the course, the student is asked to make a musical (non-verbal) response: he sings the melody he has heard and writes it down.

The course is designed to bring the student as close as possible to a lifelike musical situation. The cues and questions needed in the opening stages of the program are kept to a minimum, and are removed as soon as is practicable. While most of the melodies in the first half were written by the author, melodies from the musical literature are introduced increasingly as the course proceeds, and they predominate towards the end. Melodies are played either two or three times, not repeatedly as in much classroom dictation, and pauses between playings are limited. The student is encouraged to think quickly and to concentrate on the overall aspects of a melody, both desirable skills in listening to music in class or in concert. Finally, in order to effect a transition from hearing recorded music to hearing the sound of a "live" instrument, the Reviews and Tests are given in class by the instructor.

How does it work?

Materials for the course include a set of magnetic tapes containing all the Lessons, the student workbook, and this manual. The recorded Lessons are played on a piano, with timed intervals between playings. Reviews and Tests are not recorded. The workbook contains all necessary instructions, worksheets for all Lessons, Reviews, and Tests, answers to all Lessons and Reviews, and Student Record Sheets. This manual includes the Reviews and Tests, with instructions for their use.

The students may listen to the tapes either individually or in groups. If they work individually, they use the tapes in a listening room, language laboratory, or similar facility where the tapes may be stored and the completed worksheets collected. If students are to listen in groups, a schedule should be drawn up showing the hours at which each Lesson will be played. The learning process should not be affected by the method of organizing the listening hour, since the Lessons are timed and there is no stop once a Lesson begins.

The student brings his workbook to the listening room each time he studies a Lesson. He listens to the taped exercises, following the written and spoken instructions, and writes his responses on his worksheet. In the first half of the program, a student who reaches a specified point in the Lesson with no errors is considered to have completed the Lesson; in triple-letter Lessons, devoted to special problems, students who can complete the first of two parts without errors may omit the second part. All other students complete the entire Lesson, as instructed, and score their answers according to the instructions which are given with each Unit. They are then directed to the next Lesson. All worksheets are to be turned in to the instructor.

What does the instructor do?

The instructor should make provision for having the worksheets collected at the listening room and delivered to him. He should check the completed worksheets, first for accuracy of scoring, then—and this is more important—to see what his students are learning. In our testing of the program, the completed worksheets were very useful in identifying specific weaknesses of various students. Instructors used these worksheets as a diagnostic tool; by following up on this and comparing with students' work in allied courses, much could be learned about how to help the less proficient. Such students may need the kind of individual attention that only an instructor can provide.

The method of scoring the exercises and of establishing achievement levels for the Lessons has proved effective in the author's experience. It is recommended that these levels be adhered to the first time that an instructor uses this program. If the particular experience of a teacher shows the desirability of modifying the levels, that can be done with relative ease.

How is the program organized?

The course consists of four Units. Each Unit contains seven Lessons, a Practice Lesson, a Review, and a Test. Special Lessons devoted to specific problems are also included. Units are numbered; Lessons are lettered. A student who achieves a score of 90% in both pitch and rhythm on a single-letter Lesson moves to the next single-letter Lesson; a student who scores less than 90% in either pitch or rhythm moves to the corresponding double-letter Lesson, which is on the same level of difficulty. In the few cases where a student does not score 90% on the double-letter Lesson, he repeats the single-letter Lesson. The procedure is the same for all Lessons. A Practice Lesson is also included in each Unit; it is intended as additional drill material in preparation for the Test, for those students who wish to use it or who are assigned to do it by the instructor. The duration of a Lesson is from 15 to 30 minutes.

Relation to other courses

This program may be administered as part of a basic theory course, together with a sight singing course, or independently. In any case, the instructor who knows the content of the program will find many opportunities to relate it to other courses. Tonality and melodic structure are topics of broad interest, and are included in more than one course. For example, the instructor can relate the study of passing and neighbor tones, included in this program, to courses in harmony and counterpoint. The connection may seem obvious to the experienced musician, but it should be pointed out to the student.

Terminology

Technical terms are restricted to a small number that are in common use. The author suggests the use of sol-fa syllables (the movable Do) for singing back the melodies, since these syllables indicate tonal function. Cues and questions include the sol-fa syllables. Use of any other system is possible, such as numbers for the scale degrees.

Timetable

The amount of time required for the completion of the program depends mainly on the speed of learning. Fast classes have completed two Units in one semester, others may need an entire semester for one Unit. The author suggests that three semesters for the four Units may be the appropriate speed for an average class.

Conclusion

Born out of the need to surmount the limitations of class-room teaching, this course of programed instruction has been developed over a period of three years at Queens College. All freshman theory students during that period have taken the course. Analysis of worksheets and discussions with both students and faculty members have provided the basis for continual revision and experimentation. On the basis of experience to date, this program teaches melodic ear training successfully to at least 85% of the students—that is, they receive passing grades on the Tests. In addition, many students have reported that they received "fringe benefits" from the program, in the form of increased experience with meters, key signatures (especially in the minor mode) musical notation, rhythm, and the tonal structure of melody.

It is the author's hope and expectation that music students will find this program a useful instrument in the development of a skill which is essential for fine musicianship.

5

Some Questions and Answers About the Program

*Can the students use the tapes individually,
or must students listen in groups?*

Either one. Since the pauses between playings of the exercises are timed, the students who work individually will have no advantage or disadvantage compared to those who listen as a group.

*Should any limitations of time be imposed for the
completion of a Unit?*

Yes. Assuming that classes are fairly homogeneous, the class should be given a deadline, defined by the date set for the Review and Test. However, all classes need not be given the same deadlines.

Why are the Reviews and Tests given in class?

To begin the transfer of learning from the laboratory situation to the classroom, with the sound of the instrument itself.

Need the Reviews be graded?

No. Grading is optional, its purpose being to show the student and/or the instructor the student's progress.

Should there be any discussion of the Review in class?

By all means. Such discussions have proved quite useful in clarifying the purposes ot the course and the means used to achieve them.

What is the basis for the letter grades on the tests?

90% or over is A, each subsequent 10% less is one letter grade less. This grading may be modified by the instructor if desired.

What is the rapid-advance feature of the program?

In Units One and Two, a student who makes no errors on the first five exercises is considered to have completed the Lesson, and may proceed to the next Lesson. In this way students who are more proficient can move through the first half of the program quite rapidly without missing any of the techniques and concepts contained in those Units.

What are the prerequisites for this course?

Reading knowledge of treble and bass clefs; knowledge of major and minor scales, including key signatures; familiarity with rhythmic notations and meters.

What may the instructor do to prepare for the course?

Read through the student workbook and listen to some of the Lessons, particularly those which end each Unit (Lesson G). The more the instructor is familiar with the program, the better able he will be to adapt it to his own purposes.

Topical Outline of the Content of the Course

All melodies start on Do and on the first beat of the measure. Time signature is given. The first note of each exercise, in correct rhythmic value, is also given. Bar lines are given. Cues direct the student's attention to the contour (high and low points) of the melody. Each melody is played twice.

UNIT ONE

The taped Lessons include a Practice Lesson, which follows Lesson G. The instructor may assign the Practice Lesson as he wishes.

All melodies begin and end on Do. All start on the first beat of the measure. Time signature is given. The first note is not given. Starting with Lesson D, bar lines are no longer given. Each melody is played twice.

UNIT TWO

The taped Lessons include a Practice Lesson, which follows Lesson G. The instructor may assign the Practice Lesson as he wishes.

UNIT THREE
Melodies may begin on Do, Mi, or Sol. Most end on Do. The upbeat is introduced. The time signature is no longer given. Many melodies are in two phrases. Outlining exercises included in Lessons D, E, F, G. Each melody is played three times.

Lesson A Melodies may start on Sol; skips in the II chord; ♫♫♫ in 𝟨/𝟪

Lesson B Melodies may start on Mi; ♪.♫♫ in 𝟨/𝟪

Lesson C ♩ upbeat from Do; chromatic neighbor tone; ♩. ♫

Lesson D ♩ upbeat from Sol; chromatic double neighbor tone; syncope ♪♩ ♪

Lesson E Chromatic passing tone

Lesson F ♩ upbeat from Mi; melodies with both chromatic neighbor and passing tones

Lesson G Summary Lesson; no new material

The taped Lessons include a Practice Lesson, which follows Lesson G. The instructor may assign the Practice Lesson as he wishes.

UNIT FOUR
In addition to continuing the exercises in writing down complete melodies, Unit Four includes exercises in outlining, in detection of wrongly played notes, and in quick recognition of short melodies. Upbeats of various kinds are presented. The melodies do not increase in complexity as much as they increase in length. Melodies do not always end on Do. Each melody is played three times.

Lesson A Rests of one whole beat or more within a melody; ♫ upbeat

Lesson B ♫♫ upbeat

Lesson C Triplets within one whole beat; ³♪♩♩ upbeat

Lesson D ♪.♩ upbeat

Lesson E ♪ upbeat in 𝟤/𝟦, 𝟥/𝟦, 𝟦/𝟦

Lesson F ♪ upbeat in 𝟨/𝟪; Key of B major

Lesson G Summary Lesson; no new material

The taped Lessons include a Practice Lesson, which follows Lesson G. The instructor may assign the Practice Lesson as he wishes.

8

UNIT ONE—REVIEW

Instructions: Play each melody twice, preceding each playing with the sounding of the tonic. Allow 30 seconds after
the first playing, 45 seconds after the second.

Complete scoring instructions are given in the student
workbook.

UNIT ONE—TEST

Instructions: Play each melody twice, preceding each playing with the sounding of the tonic.   Allow 30 seconds after
the first playing, 45 seconds after the second.

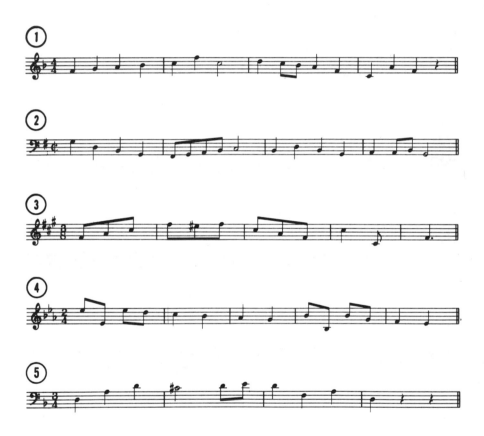

Scoring: Mark x over any incorrect pitch, and x under any
beat that is not rhythmically correct. Total all x's and subtract from 109, as indicated on student worksheet.   This
gives numerical score. Conversion to letter grades is
given below. For your convenience, a box is provided on
the worksheet for entering the letter grades.

A 109-98   B 97-87   C 86-76   D 75-65

UNIT TWO—REVIEW

Instructions: Play each melody twice, preceding each playing with the sounding of the tonic. Allow 30 seconds after the first playing, 45 seconds after the second.

Complete scoring instructions are given in the student workbook.

UNIT TWO—TEST

Instructions: Play each melody twice, preceding each play-ing with the sounding of the tonic. Allow 30 seconds after the first playing, 45 after the second.

Scoring: Mark x over any incorrect pitch and x under any beat that is not rhythmically correct. Total all x's and sub-tract from 157, as indicated on the student worksheet. This gives numerical score. Conversion to letter grades is given below. For your convenience, a box is provided on the work-sheet for entering the letter grade.

A 157-142   B 141-126   C 125-110   D 109-93

UNIT THREE—REVIEW

Instructions: Play each melody *three* times, preceding each playing with the sounding of the tonic. Allow 30 seconds after the first playing, 45 seconds after the second, and one minute after the third.

Complete scoring instructions are given on the student workbook. NOTE: Rhythmic notation in parentheses may be considered correct.

UNIT THREE—TEST

Instructions: Play each melody *three* times, preceding each playing with the sounding of the tonic. Allow 30 seconds after the first playing, 45 seconds after the second, and one minute after the third.

Scoring: Mark x over any incorrect pitch and a under any beat that is not rhythmically correct. Total all x's and subtract from 196, as indicated on the student worksheet. This gives numerical score. Conversion to letter grades is given below. For your convenience, a box is provided on the worksheet for entering the letter grade.

A 225-203   B 202-180   C 179-158   D 157-135

UNIT FOUR—REVIEW

Instructions: Play each melody *three* times, preceding each playing with the sounding of the tonic. Allow 30 seconds after the first playing, 45 seconds after the second, and one minute after the third.

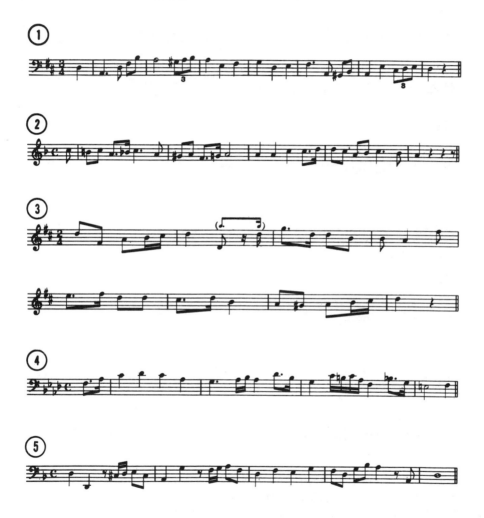

Complete scoring instructions are given on the student worksheet.

UNIT FOUR—TEST

Instructions: Play each melody *three* times, preceding each playing with the sounding of the tonic. Allow 30 seconds after the first playing, 45 seconds after the second, and one minute after the third.

Scoring: Mark x over any incorrect pitch and x under any beat that is not rhythmically correct. Total all x's and subtract from 241, as indicated on the student worksheet. This gives numerical score. Conversion to letter grades is given below. For your convenience, a box is provided on the worksheet for entering the letter grade.

A 241-218   B 217-194   C 193-170   D 169-146

The same procedure is followed as in the double-letter Lessons, except that there are only five exercises. Each melody, preceded by the preliminary note (tonic), is played twice.

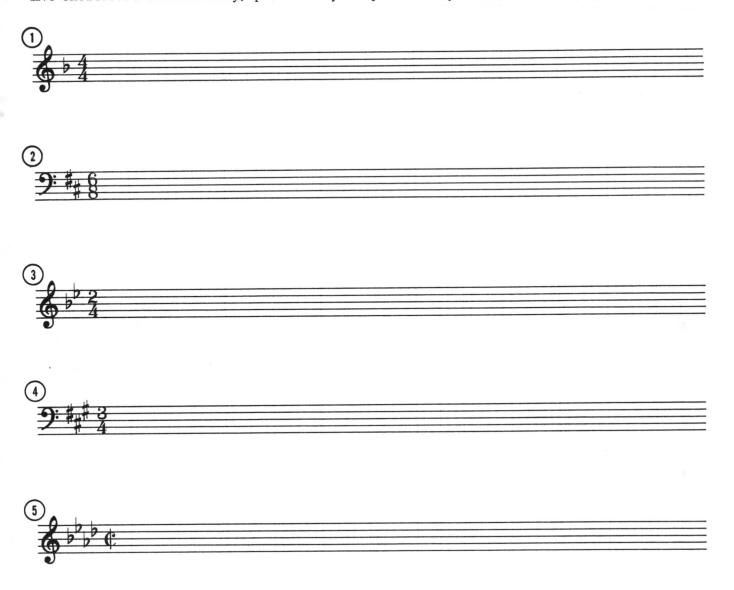

To find the correct answers to Exercises 1-3, tear the worksheet UP from the bottom along the perforation, and fold along the dotted line. Find the correct answers to 4 and 5 by tearing DOWN from the top and folding along the dashed line. Add pitch x's and rhythm x's for total number of errors.

Scoring: 154

           -         (total x)

_____(score)   CONVERSION TO LETTER GRADES ON REVERSE

Conversion to letter grades:

A: 154-140

B: 139-125

C: 124-110

D: 109- 95

The same procedure is followed as in the double-letter Lessons and the Review; there are only five exercises. Each melody, preceded by the preliminary note (tonic), is played twice.

① (treble clef, 1 flat, common time — empty staff)

② (treble clef, 1 flat, 3/4 — empty staff)

③ (bass clef, 1 sharp, cut time — empty staff)

④ (treble clef, 3 sharps, 6/8 — empty staff)

⑤ (treble clef, 3 flats, 3/4 — empty staff)

Scoring: 157

—   (total x)

————   (score)

UNIT THREE

III III III III III III III III III III III III III

STUDENT RECORD SHEET

Circle the Lesson you are to do next.

After completing that Lesson, draw a line through the circle, and circle the Lesson the instructions tell you to do next.

Keep this sheet up to date. It is intended solely for your guidance.

Ⓐ   AA   AAA

B   BB

C   CC

D   DD   DDD

E   EE

F   FF

G   GG

Starting date _____

Completion date _____

HOW TO STUDY UNIT THREE: LESSONS A—C

Single-Letter Lessons

Although the procedure in these Lessons is divided into two parts, the parts both employ the same material, and consequently the same worksheet. The illustrations at the top of the worksheet are played at the beginning of Part 2.

Part 1

a. The five melodies comprising the Lesson are each played *once* at 20-second intervals, preceded by the preliminary note (tonic). Concentrate on the mode and meter; quickly write the time signature and, at the end of the line, the last note (by writing the last note, you define the mode, since the last note is always Do unless otherwise specified). If you can write any other notes or cues in the 20 seconds, do so.

b. After the fifth melody has been played, there is a one-minute pause, during which you check your answers to Part 1. For the correct answers, fold the worksheet from the right side to the dashed line on the back. Check your answers (do not score). If any of your time signatures or last notes is not correct, you may change it at this point. Then proceed to Part 2. (NOTE: In this course you are not expected to distinguish between $\frac{2}{4}$, ¢, and $\frac{4}{4}$, nor between $\frac{3}{8}$ and $\frac{6}{8}$.)

Part 2

c. The illustration at the top of the worksheet (if any) is now played.

d. Each melody, preceded by the preliminary note (the tonic), is now played twice, with a 30-second pause after the first playing and a 45-second pause after the second playing. After the first playing, sing back the tune, beating time as you sing, and write down as much of the melody as you can. Use the second hearing to complete and check your answer. Procedure is the same for each exercise.

e. After Exercise 5, mark your answers to Part 2. For correct answers to Exercises 1-3, tear the worksheet UP from the bottom and fold along the dotted line. When you have marked 1-3, find the correct answers to 4 and 5 by tearing DOWN from the top and folding along the dashed line. Mark and score your answers according to the following instructions.

Scoring (for full details, see p. 6):

- Mark x *over* any incorrect pitch.
- Mark x *under* any incorrect beat. (Do not score rests.)
- If you select the wrong first note but write the melody correctly relative to that note, write 5 x's *over* the first note.
- Add up the number of pitch x's (*over* the notes) in the Lesson and enter in the space marked: (Px).
- Add up the number of rhythm x's (*under* the notes) in the Lesson and enter in the space marked: (Rx).
- Subtract from the given figures to obtain your pitch score (P-score) and rhythm score (R-score).

f. Turn the worksheet over to find the next instruction. Mark your Student Record Sheet accordingly, sign the worksheet, remove it, and hand it in.

Double-Letter Lessons

In this part of the course, the double-letter Lessons are done in the same way as the single-letter Lessons. Follow the procedure above.

Triple-Letter Lesson

Instructions for Lesson AAA are given on the worksheet. This Lesson comprises additional drill in rapid discrimination of meter.

NOTE: If there are any Lessons that you do not have to do, tear them out so that this instruction page will always conveniently face the worksheet you are using.

Basic Conducting Patterns

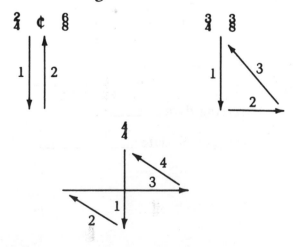

We have studied the Do-La-Fa-Re pattern . . . and the Do-Fa-La . . .. Here is Re-Fa-La, the outline of the II chord.

①

. . . . The familiar Sol-Le-Sol NT pattern may be elaborated with chordal skips between the NT. As a step towards long-range listening, try to keep in mind the NT figure while hearing the embellishing notes in between.

②

③ This melody starts on Sol. From this point on, melodies may start on Do or Sol. The preliminary note is always Do.

④ When ♩. is the unit, a beat may include ♪♫♫

⑤ This melody consists of two phrases. The first has a definite goal. Listen for it and jot it down. The second phrase is similar to the first, but not identical.

Scoring
of Part 2:   117   69

          -      (Px)   -   (Rx)

          _____ (P-score) _____ (R-score)

If you have made any error
in identification of meter,
proceed to Lesson AAA before going on.

NEXT INSTRUCTION ON REVERSE

PART 1

If P-score is 105 or more
AND R-score is 62 or more,
proceed to Lesson B;
otherwise, proceed to AA.

PART 2

As you listen for the mode and meter, try to hear more than just the last note. Many melodies end with familiar patterns which you can recognize at once. Reminder: melodies may begin on Sol or Do.

① (treble clef, two sharps)

② (bass clef, three flats)

③ This excerpt from Brahms's Violin Concerto does not end on Do. Write the last note and the name of its scale degree.

(bass clef, two sharps)

④ Identify the goal at the midpoint of this bass line by Bach.

(bass clef, one sharp)

(bass clef, one sharp)

⑤ (treble clef, three sharps)

(treble clef, two sharps)

Scoring
of Part 2:   108   60

          -    (Px)   -   (Rx)

If you have made any error
in identification of meter,
proceed to Lesson AAA before going on.

_____ (P-score)   _____ (R-score)   NEXT INSTRUCTION ON REVERSE

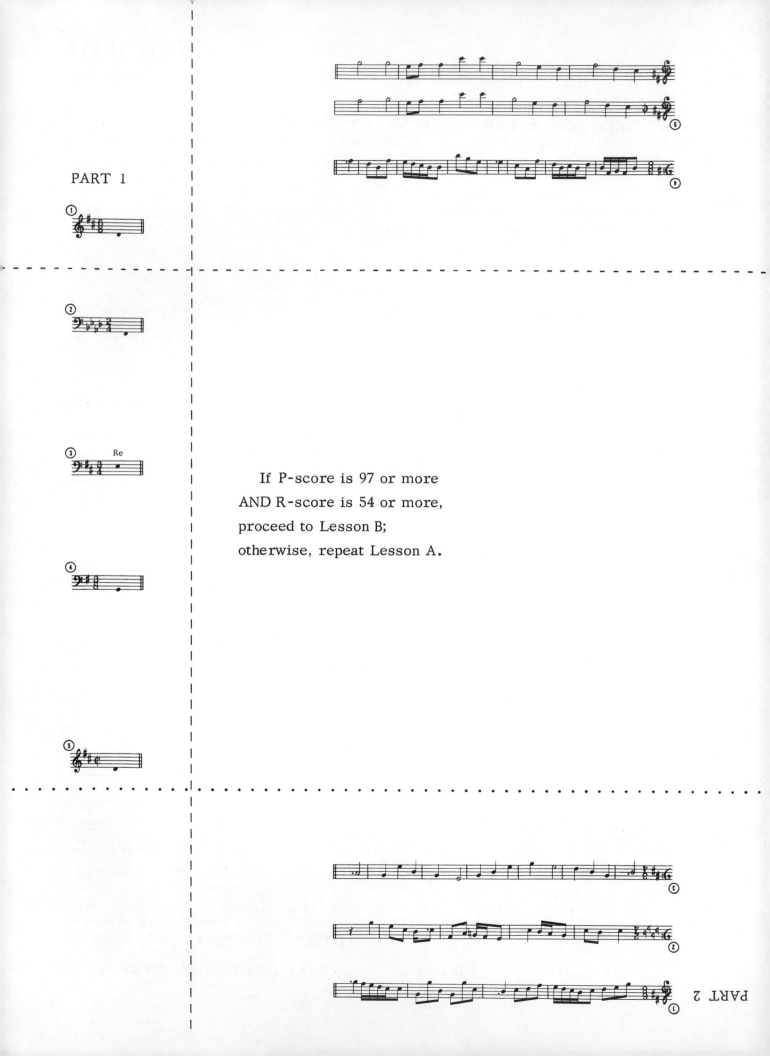

PART 1

If P-score is 97 or more
AND R-score is 54 or more,
proceed to Lesson B;
otherwise, repeat Lesson A.

This Lesson is devoted to drill in recognizing meters. Even in these brief exercises you will find it useful to sing back the tune and beat time as you sing. The exercises consist of melody excerpts, played once each, without preliminary note. Write your answers, the number of beats in a measure, in the spaces below. The answers will be 2, 3, or 4. Some of the exercises are in $\frac{6}{8}$ time, and some in $\frac{3}{8}$. Although either 2 or 3 will be considered correct for a melody in $\frac{6}{8}$, such an answer will not be very helpful when you have to write out the melody in later Lessons. Try to identify $\frac{3}{8}$ and $\frac{6}{8}$ in this Lesson. All answers which are considered correct are included on the answer page.

PART 1.

1. _____ 2. _____ 3. _____ 4. _____ 5. _____

6. _____ 7. _____ 8. _____ 9. _____ 10. _____

You now have one minute to score. Fold this sheet up from the bottom to see the answers to Part 1. Mark x through any answer which is not correct.

If all ten are correct, proceed to the Lesson previously indicated. If there are any errors, resume this Lesson.

PART 2.

1. _____ 2. _____ 3. _____ 4. _____ 5. _____

6. _____ 7. _____ 8. _____ 9. _____ 10. _____

Fold this sheet down from the top to see the answers to Part 2. Mark x through any incorrect answer.

Now proceed to the Lesson previously indicated.

PART 1: 1. 3   2. **2**(4)   3. **4**   4. $\frac{6}{8}$(2, $\frac{3}{8}$, 3)   5. 3

6. **2**(4)   7. $\frac{3}{8}$($\frac{6}{8}$, 3)   8. **2**(4)   9. **4**   10. $\frac{6}{8}$($\frac{3}{8}$, 2, 3)

- -

PART 2: 1. 3   2. **2**(4)   3. **4**   4. **2**(4)   5. $\frac{6}{8}$($\frac{3}{8}$, 2)

6. **3**   7. **4**(2)   8. $\frac{3}{8}$($\frac{6}{8}$, 3)   9. **4**   10. $\frac{6}{8}$(2, 3)

Melodies may start on Do, Mi (Me), or Sol. The preliminary note is always Do.

① Listen for the difference in the endings of the two phrases that make up this melody by Beethoven.

② When $\downarrow.$ is the unit, a beat may include ♩. ♫♫

③ This Haydn minuet begins with a $\downarrow$ upbeat.

④

⑤ The last note of this Mozart excerpt is not Do. Write the last note and the name of its scale degree.

Scoring
of Part 2:   118   84

            -        (Px)   -   (Rx)

        _____(P-score)   _____(R-score)   NEXT INSTRUCTION ON REVERSE

PART 1

If P-score is 106 or more
AND R-score is 76 or more,
proceed to Lesson C;
otherwise, proceed to BB.

PART 2

① Remember that a melody may begin on Do, Mi (Me), or Sol. This melody does not end on Do. Write the last note and its scale degree.

②

③ Listen for the connection between the opening note and a NT which follows soon after.

④ This melody from a Beethoven sonata does not end on Do. Write the last note and its scale degree.

⑤

Scoring
of Part 2:   98   57

         -    (Px)   -   (Rx)

      —————(P-score)   —————(R-score)   NEXT INSTRUCTION ON REVERSE

PART 1

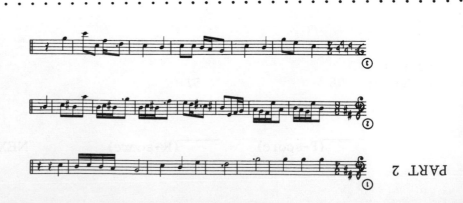

① Sol

②

If P-score is 88 or more
AND R-score is 51 or more,
proceed to Lesson C;
otherwise, repeat Lesson B.

③

④ Mi

⑤

PART 2

As an elaboration of Do-Mi-Sol-Do we hear. . . . The first NT is part of the diatonic scale, as previous NT have been. The other two are chromatic. Sharps, double sharps, and natural signs may be required to spell chromatic NT.

①   Indicate the notes on the strong beat, which are embellished with NT.

②   The melody begins with a ♩ upbeat. From this point, upbeats are included when the unit is ♩

An elaboration of the rhythm ♩. ♪♩ may be ♩. ♫♩ The illustration is from Mozart's Oboe Quartet.

③   The melody does not end on Do. Write the last pitch and its scale degree.

④   Mark the notes that fall on the strong beat.

⑤   What is the goal at midpoint?

Scoring
of Part 2:   103   80

      -       (Px)   -   (Rx)

          _____ (P-score)   _____ (R-score)   NEXT INSTRUCTION ON REVERSE

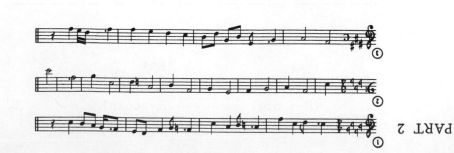

PART 1

If P-score is 93 or more
AND R-score is 72 or more,
proceed to Lesson D;
otherwise, proceed to CC.

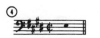

Name:

Date: Instructor:

① The melody starts on: Do? Mi? Me? Sol?

② This melody by Purcell does not end on Do. Write down the note and the name of its scale degree.

③

④ Repetition of the rhythmic motive is a clue to the meter of this tune by Vivaldi.

⑤

Scoring
of Part 2:   120   68

        -    (Px)   -   (Rx)

    _____ (P-score)   _____ (R-score)   NEXT INSTRUCTION ON REVERSE

PART 1

①

② Mi

③

If P-score is 108 or more
AND R-score is 61 or more,
proceed to Lesson D;
otherwise, repeat Lesson C.

④

⑤

PART 2

TURN THIS PAGE FOR NEW INSTRUCTIONS
FOR THE REMAINING LESSONS IN UNIT THREE

HOW TO STUDY UNIT THREE: LESSONS D—G

Single-Letter Lessons

In these Lessons, Parts 1 and 2 are on separate worksheets.

Part 1

Starting with Lesson D, a new technique is introduced, designed to help you hear longer melodic connections. Instead of trying to hear every note, you concentrate on those notes that outline the melodies. These notes are indicated on the worksheet by cues showing the beats where they occur. Arrows (↑) below the staff indicate these beats; the marks (|) above the staff indicate all the beats in a measure, in cases where the note required is not on the first beat; the beamed arrows (⊔) mean two adjacent notes in the melody. An illustration of the technique is given at the beginning of Lesson D, Part 1.

a. Each melody is played *once*, preceded by the preliminary note (the tonic). Outline as indicated. There is a 15-second pause after each melody.

b. After the last melody in Part 1, there is a one-minute pause, during which you check your answers. For the correct answers, tear the worksheet UP from the bottom along the perforation, and fold along the dotted line. Check your answers (do not score), then turn to the next worksheet and proceed with Part 2.

Part 2

c. Each melody, preceded by the preliminary note (the tonic), is played *three* times, with a 30-second pause after the first playing, 45 seconds after the second, and one minute after the third. Make use of outlining technique where you can. Note that, from this point on, not all melodies end on Do.

d. After Exercise 5, mark your answers to Part 2. For correct answers to Exercises 1-3, tear the worksheet UP from the bottom and fold along the dotted line. When you have marked 1-3, find the correct answers to 4 and 5 by tearing DOWN from the top and folding along the dashed line. Mark and score

your answers according to the following instructions.

Scoring (For full details, see p. 6):

- Mark x over any incorrect pitch.
- Mark x under any incorrect beat. (Do not score rests.)
- If you select the wrong first note but write the melody correctly relative to that note, write 5 x's over the first note.
- If your answer is written in the wrong meter, write 5 x's under the time signature (but remember that you are not expected to distinguish between $\frac{2}{4}$, ¢, and $\frac{4}{4}$, nor between $\frac{3}{8}$ and $\frac{6}{8}$; your answer is correct in these cases if your notation of the melody is correct relative to your time signature).
- Add up the number of pitch x's (*over* the notes) in the Lesson and enter in the space marked: (Px).
- Add up the number of rhythm x's (*under* the notes) in the Lesson and enter in the space marked: (Rx).
- Subtract from the given figures to obtain your pitch score (P-score) and rhythm score (R-score).

e. Turn the worksheet over to find the next instruction. Mark your Student Record Sheet accordingly, sign both worksheets, remove them, and hand them in.

Double-Letter Lessons

Outlining exercises are not included in double-letter Lessons. Follow the procedure for Part 2 of the single-letter Lessons (steps c-e above).

Triple-Letter Lesson

Instructions for Lesson DDD are given on the worksheet. This Lesson comprises additional drill in rapid discrimination of meter and recognition of upbeats.

NOTE: If there are any Lessons that you do not have to do, tear them out so that this instruction page will always conveniently face the worksheet you are using.

Part 1 consists of exercises in hearing connections between notes which are not adjacent in the melody, which will be called long-range connections. Instead of trying to hear all of the notes, concentrate on certain ones which may be considered as the outline of the melody. Cues to these notes are given. You have already heard such long-range connections, as when the NT Sol-Le-Sol . . . is elaborated by the use of intervening notes . . . By focusing upon the connections, you may be able to grasp and retain longer melodic segments, particularly if they are sequential.

The cue that tells you where the noteheads are to be written is ↑, as in the illustration below. The mark ⏐ indicates beats within a measure, where the note required is not on the first beat. ⎣⎦ means two adjacent notes in the melody.

Now listen to the illustration, which has been outlined below. Follow the outline as the illustration is played. The preliminary note is always Do.

Outline the two melodies you will now hear. Each one is played once.

AFTER CHECKING PART 1, TURN TO THE NEXT WORKSHEET AND PROCEED WITH PART 2.

From this point, not all melodies end on Do. ♩ upbeats may begin on Sol or Do.

① Two long phrases make up this melody by Brahms. There is a clear point of rest (goal) at the end of the first phrase.

② This melody by Bellini introduces the syncopated rhythm ♪♩ ♪

③

④ A tune by Smetana, in which the DN figure includes one chromatic NT.

⑤

Scoring
of Part 2:   131   86

          -      (Px)   -   (Rx)

          _____ (P-score)   _____ (R-score)   NEXT INSTRUCTION ON REVERSE

If P-score is 118 or more
AND R-score is 77 or more,
proceed to Lesson E;
otherwise, proceed to DD.

Alternate rhythmic notation given in parentheses may also be considered correct.

① Chromatic NT are included in the NT figure. Outline this melody.

②

③

④ Use eighth rests in this melody by Bach.

⑤ Listen for the goal at the midpoint of this tune by Beethoven.

Scoring: 106   75

          -      (Px)   -   (Rx)

          _____(P-score)   _____(R-score)   NEXT INSTRUCTION ON REVERSE

If P-score is 95 or more
AND R-score is 67 or more,
proceed to Lesson E;
otherwise, repeat Lesson D.

This Lesson contains drills in recognizing meters when the melody begins with an upbeat. Some of the melodies begin on the first beat of the measure, but some begin with an eighth or quarter note upbeat. Even in these brief exercises you will find it useful to sing back the tune and beat time as you sing. The exercises consist of melody excerpts, played once each, without preliminary note. Answer two questions about each melody: is there an upbeat, what is the meter? Each exercise number is followed by   up   . If you hear an upbeat, cross out
                                                                        down
down. If you don't hear an upbeat, cross out up. Based on the same single playing, determine the meter. Write your answers, the number of beats in a measure, in the spaces below. The answers will be 2, 3, or 4. Exercises in $\frac{3}{8}$ and $\frac{6}{8}$ are included. Although either 2 or 3 will be considered correct for a melody in $\frac{6}{8}$, such an answer will not be very helpful when you have to write out the melody in later Lessons. Try to identify $\frac{3}{8}$ and $\frac{6}{8}$ in this Lesson. All answers which are considered correct are included on the answer page.

PART 1.

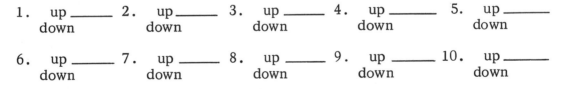

1. up _____ 2. up _____ 3. up _____ 4. up _____ 5. up _____
    down   down   down   down   down

6. up _____ 7. up _____ 8. up _____ 9. up _____ 10. up _____
    down   down   down   down   down

You now have one minute to score. Fold this sheet up from the bottom to see the answers to Part 1. Mark x through any answer which is not correct.

If all ten are correct, proceed to the Lesson previously indicated. If there are any errors, resume this Lesson.

PART 2.

1. up _____ 2. up _____ 3. up _____ 4. up _____ 5. up _____
    down   down   down   down   down

6. up _____ 7. up _____ 8. up _____ 9. up _____ 10. up _____
    down   down   down   down   down

Fold this sheet down from the top to see answers to Part 2. Mark x through any incorrect answer.

Now proceed to the Lesson to which you were previously directed.

PART 1.

1. up 3   2. down 3   3. up 4   4. down 2 (4)   5. up $\frac{6}{8}$ (2, 3)

6. up 3   7. up $\frac{3}{8}$ ($\frac{6}{8}$, 3)   8. down 2 (4)   9. up 4   10. up $\frac{6}{8}$ (2, 3)

PART 2.

1. up 3   2. down 4   3. down 2 (4)   4. down $\frac{3}{8}$ ($\frac{6}{8}$, 3)   5. down 3

6. up 2 (4)   7. up $\frac{6}{8}$ ($\frac{3}{8}$, 2, 3)   8. up 3   9. down 2 (4)   10. down 4

Outline on one hearing.

①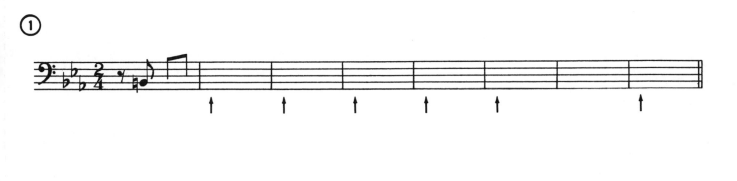

②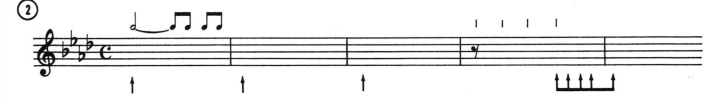

AFTER CHECKING PART 1, TURN TO THE NEXT WORKSHEET AND PROCEED WITH PART 2.

① The PT in bar 2 fills the space between Sol and Fa. It is not a note of the diatonic scale. It is a chromatic PT.

②

③ A rest is required after the first phrase of this melody by Pergolesi.

④

⑤ Can the outlining technique of Part I be applied to any part of this melody by Haydn?

Scoring
of Part 2:   127   105

         -      (Px)   -   (Rx)

_____(P-score)   _____(R-score)   NEXT INSTRUCTION ON REVERSE

If P-score is 114 or more
AND R-score is 94 or more,
proceed to Lesson F;
otherwise, proceed to EE.

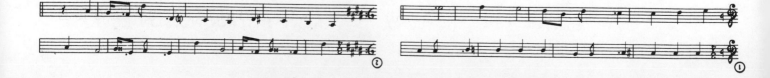

① Cue in scale passage.

② Can outlining be used on any part of this melody?

③

④ Listen for repetition.

⑤

Scoring: 125   100

           -        (Px)   -   (Rx)

        _____(P-score)   _____(R-score)   NEXT INSTRUCTION ON REVERSE

If P-score is 112 or more
AND R-score is 90 or more,
proceed to Lesson F;
otherwise, repeat Lesson E.

Outline on one hearing.

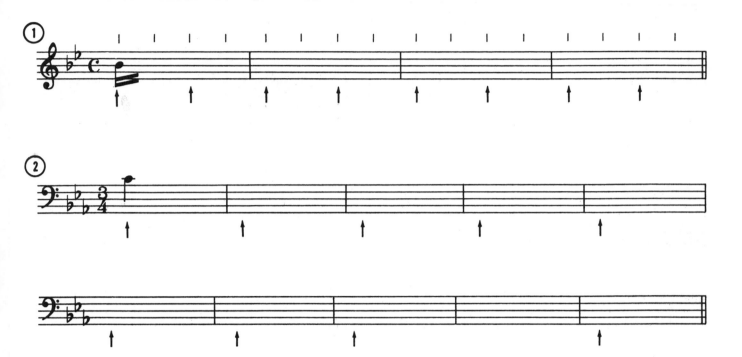

AFTER CHECKING PART 1, TURN TO THE NEXT WORKSHEET AND PROCEED WITH PART 2.

A melody may include both chromatic NT and chromatic PT. The ♩ upbeat may start from Do, Mi (Me), or Sol.

①   The two phrases of this German folk tune are separated by a quarter rest.

②

③   The first part of the melody centers around: Do? Me? Sol?

④

⑤   Apply outlining technique to this Handel bass line.

Scoring
of Part 2:   112   89

         -     (Px)   -   (Rx)

           _____ (P-score)   _____ (R-score)   NEXT INSTRUCTION ON REVERSE

If P-score is 101 or more
AND R-score is 80 or more,
proceed to Lesson G;
otherwise, proceed to FF.

Do not score rests in Unit Three.

①   Indicate high and low points in this robust tune by Grétry.

②

③   Outlining technique can be applied to this melody.

④

⑤   Note the goal at the midpoint of this Haydn melody.

Scoring: 130   110

         -        (Px)   -   (Rx)

        _____ (P-score)   _____ (R-score)   NEXT INSTRUCTION ON REVERSE

If P-score is 117 or more
AND R-score is 99 or more,
proceed to Lesson G;
otherwise, repeat Lesson F.

Outline on one hearing.

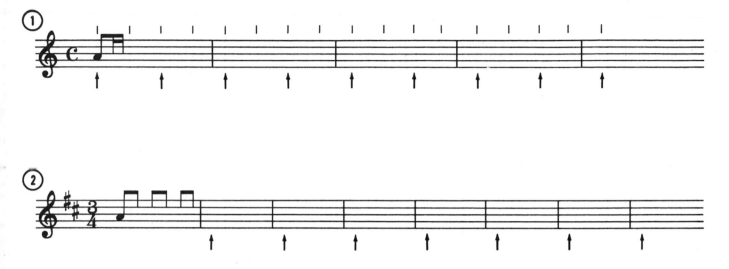

AFTER CHECKING PART 1, TURN TO THE NEXT WORKSHEET AND PROCEED WITH PART 2.

This is a summary Lesson. No new material is introduced, and there are no cues. Use outlining technique where you can.

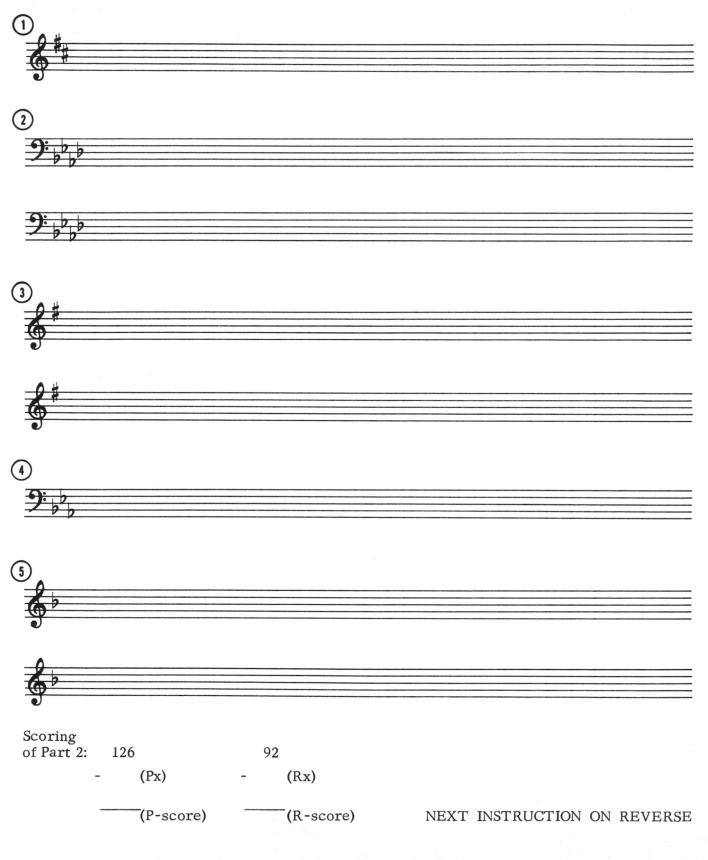

Scoring
of Part 2:   126   92

          -      (Px)   -   (Rx)

          _____(P-score)   _____(R-score)   NEXT INSTRUCTION ON REVERSE

If P-score is 113 or more
AND R-score is 83 or more,
you have completed Unit Three;
otherwise proceed to Lesson GG.
A Practice Lesson is available after G or GG.

Name:

Date: Instructor:

This Lesson reviews upbeats, chromatic PT and NT, repetition of both pitch and rhythm patterns.

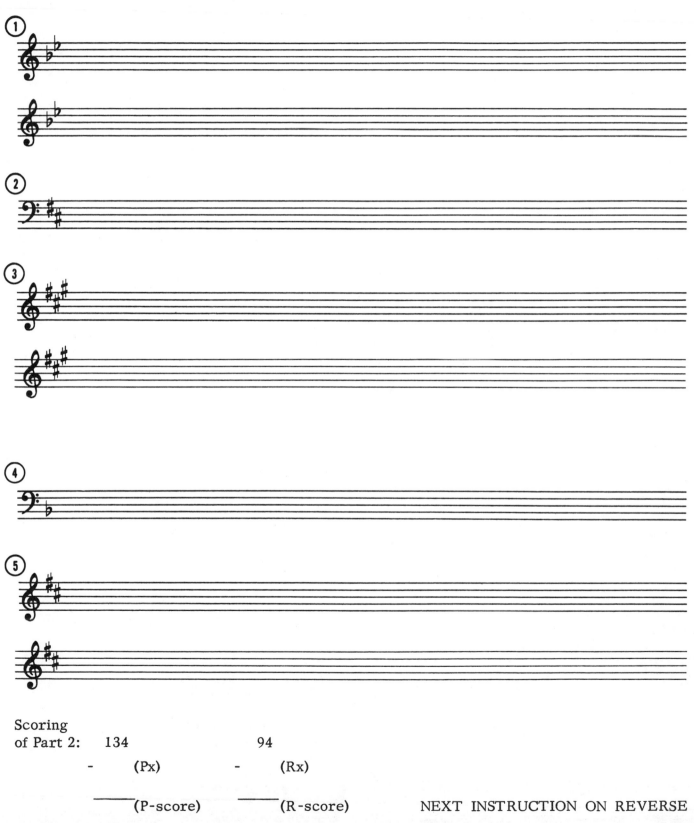

Scoring
of Part 2:   134   94

         -    (Px)   -   (Rx)

_____ (P-score) _____ (R-score)   NEXT INSTRUCTION ON REVERSE

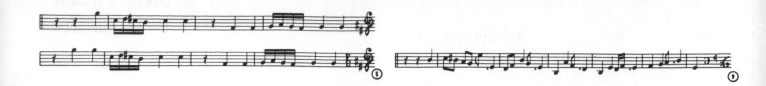

If P-score is 121 or more
AND R-score is   85 or more,
you have completed Unit Three;
otherwise, repeat Lesson G.
A Practice Lesson is available after GG.

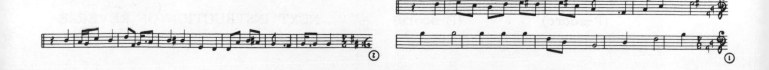

The same procedure is followed as in the double-letter Lessons. Each melody, preceded by the preliminary note (tonic), is played three times.

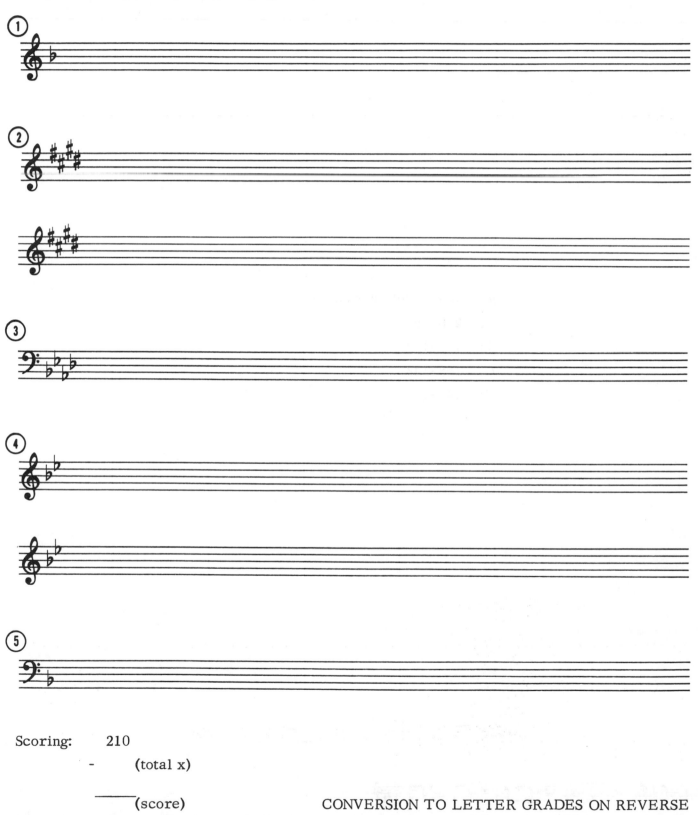

Scoring: 210

-          (total x)

_____ (score)   CONVERSION TO LETTER GRADES ON REVERSE

Conversion to letter grades:

A: 210-190
B: 189-169
C: 168-148
D: 147-127

The same procedure is followed as in the double-letter Lessons. Each melody, preceded by the preliminary note (tonic), is played three times.

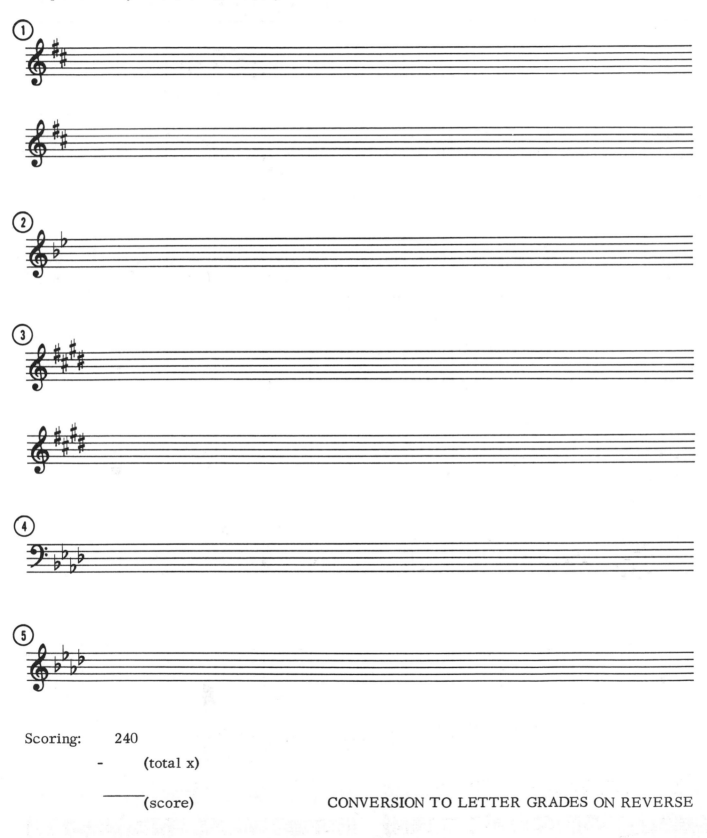

Scoring: 240

      -        (total x)

_____ (score)   CONVERSION TO LETTER GRADES ON REVERSE

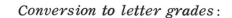

Conversion to letter grades:

    A: 240-217

    B: 216-193

    C: 192-169

    D: 168-145

The same procedure is followed as in the double-letter Lessons and the Review. Each melody, preceded by the preliminary note (tonic), is played three times.

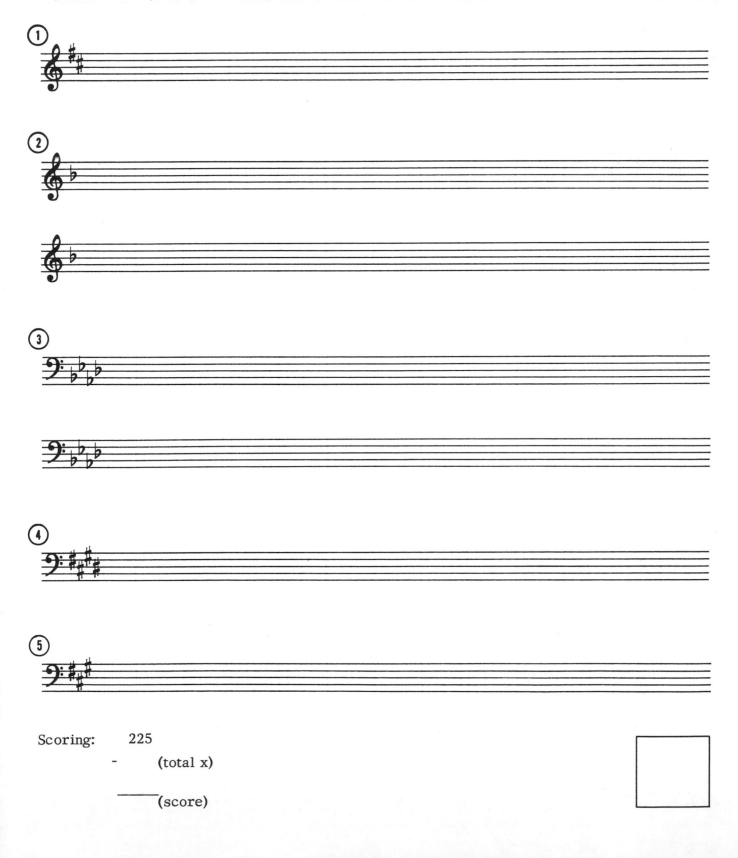

Scoring: 225

         -          (total x)

         _____(score)

UNIT FOUR

IIII IIII IIII IIII IIII IIII IIII IIII

STUDENT RECORD SHEET

Circle the Lesson you are to do next.

After completing that Lesson, draw a line through the circle, and circle the Lesson the instructions tell you to do next.

Keep this sheet up to date. It is intended solely for your guidance.

(A)   AA

B   BB

C   CC

D   DD

E   EE

F   FF

G   GG

Starting date _____

Completion date _____

HOW TO STUDY UNIT FOUR

Single-Letter Lessons: A—F

Part 1

a. In this Unit, Part 1 includes several different types of exercise, and specific instructions are given on each worksheet.

b. After the exercises of Part 1, there is a one-minute pause, during which you check your answers. For the correct answers, tear the worksheet UP from the bottom along the perforation, and fold along the dotted line. Check your answers (do not score), then turn to the next worksheet and proceed with Part 2.

Part 2

c. Each melody, preceded by the preliminary note (the tonic), is played *three* times, with a 30-second pause after the first playing, 45 seconds after the second, and one minute after the third. Make use of outlining technique where you can.

d. After Exercise 5, mark your answers to Part 2. For correct answers to Exercises 1-3, tear the worksheet UP from the bottom and fold along the dotted line. When you have marked 1-3, find the correct answers to 4 and 5 by tearing DOWN from the top and folding along the dashed line. Mark and score your answers according to the following instructions.

Scoring (for full details, see p. 6):

- Mark x *over* any incorrect pitch.
- Mark x *under* any incorrect beat.
- Score rests whose value is one full beat or more (when rests of less than one beat occur, the correct answers give alternative readings, any one of which is acceptable).

- If you select the wrong first note but write the melody correctly relative to that note, write 5 x's *over* the first note.
- If your answer is written in the wrong meter write 5 x's *under* the time signature (but remember that you are not expected to distinguish between $\frac{2}{4}$, $\mathȼ$, and $\frac{4}{4}$, nor between $\frac{3}{8}$ and $\frac{6}{8}$; your answer is correct in these cases if your notation of the melody is correct relative to your time signature).
- Add up the number of pitch x's (*over* the notes) in the Lesson and enter in the space marked: (Px).
- Add up the number of rhythm x's (*under* the notes) in the Lesson and enter in the space marked: (Rx).
- Subtract from the given figures to obtain your pitch score (P-score) and rhythm score (R-score).

e. Turn the worksheet over to find the next instruction. Mark your Student Record Sheet accordingly, sign both worksheets, remove them, and hand them in.

Lesson G & Double-Letter Lessons

There is only one part to these Lessons. Follow the procedure for Part 2 of the two-part Lessons (steps c-e above).

NOTE: If there are any Lessons that you do not have to do, tear them out so that this instruction page will always conveniently face the worksheet you are doing.

Name:

Date: Instructor:

In Unit Four, outlining is continued, but with fewer cues. As an illustration of how much in-
formation can be heard by listening to longer connections and being alert to melodic techniques already studied, here is a melody from Mozart's *Jupiter Symphony*. An outline and
cues are given, such as you might jot down on first hearing of the melody. After you hear the
excerpt, fill in as many notes as you can. The melody will be repeated in 30 seconds. The
complete melody is included in the answers to Part 1.

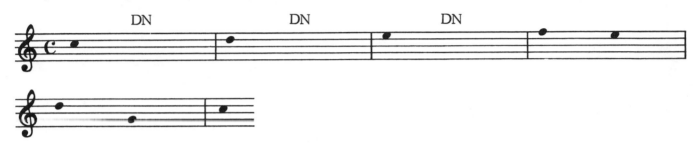

①   Outline this melody, which has two levels of stepwise connection. Listen for the
      highest and lowest notes in each group of the sequence.

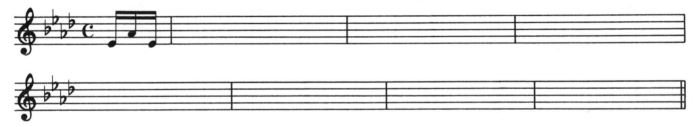

②   Again two levels are suggested by the melody, but in a different way. Both levels
      reach their goals at the same time.

Illustration

Use outlining technique where possible. Many melodies will be in two phrases. Listen for the goal of the first phrase and jot it down as you hear it.

Upbeats may include ♫ From this point, score rests when they are equal to one or more beats. When they are less than one beat in value, do not score.

① The two phrases are separated by a rest.

②

③

④

⑤

Scoring
of Part 2:   118   78

         -      (Px)   -   (Rx)

_____ (P-score)   _____ (R-score)   NEXT INSTRUCTION ON REVERSE

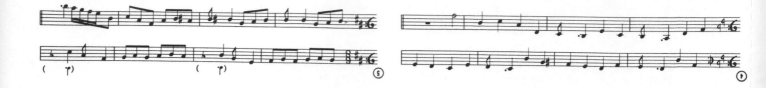

If P-score is 106 or more
AND R-score is 70 or more,
proceed to Lesson B;
otherwise, proceed to AA.

Name:

Date: Instructor:

①

②

③ The first part of the melody centers around: Do? Mi? Sol?

④ The goal at mid-point?

⑤

Scoring: 121   95

        -      (Px)   -   (Rx)

_____(P-score)   _____(R-score)   NEXT INSTRUCTION ON REVERSE

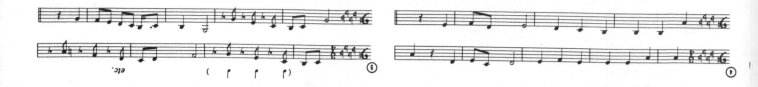

If P-score is 109 or more
AND R-score is 86 or more,
proceed to Lesson B;
otherwise, repeat Lesson A.

Three short melodies will be heard, once each. Memorize each melody as you hear it, and sing it back. Then write it down. There are 30 seconds between melodies. The preliminary note is always Do, and cues are given. After completing Part 1, fold this sheet up from the bottom and check your answers. Do not score.

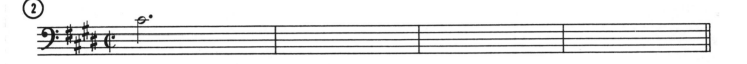

Upbeats may now include  Melodies may begin and end on any note of the scale.

①

②

③ A grace note is heard near the end of this Haydn minuet. Do not score the grace note.

④

⑤

Scoring
of Part 2:   162   94

         -      (Px)   -   (Rx)

_____ (P-score)   _____ (R-score)   NEXT INSTRUCTION ON REVERSE

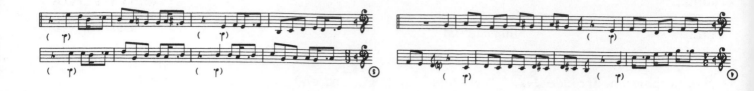

If P-score is 146 or more
AND R-score is 85 or more,
proceed to Lesson C;
otherwise, proceed to BB.

Name:

Date: Instructor:

UNIT FOUR
Lesson BB

①

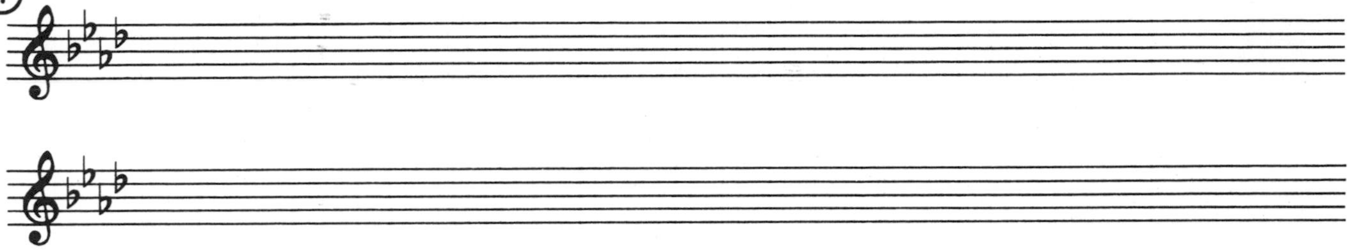

②

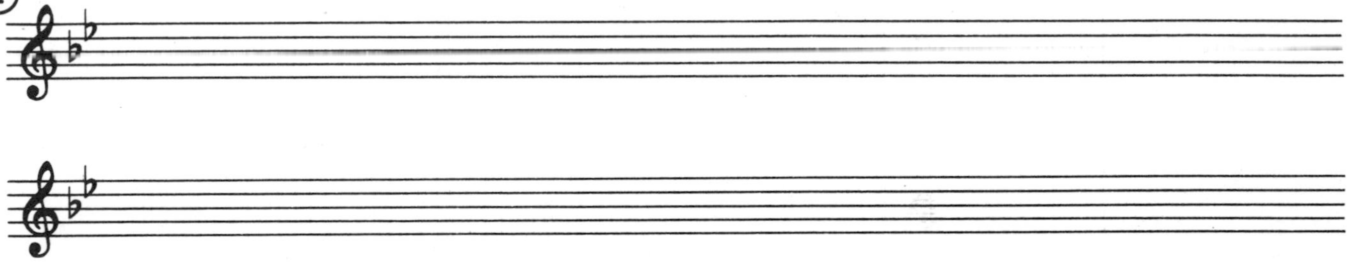

③

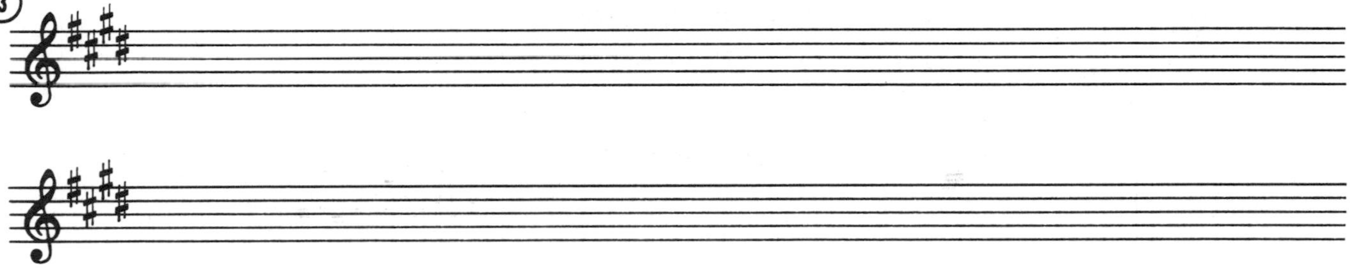

④

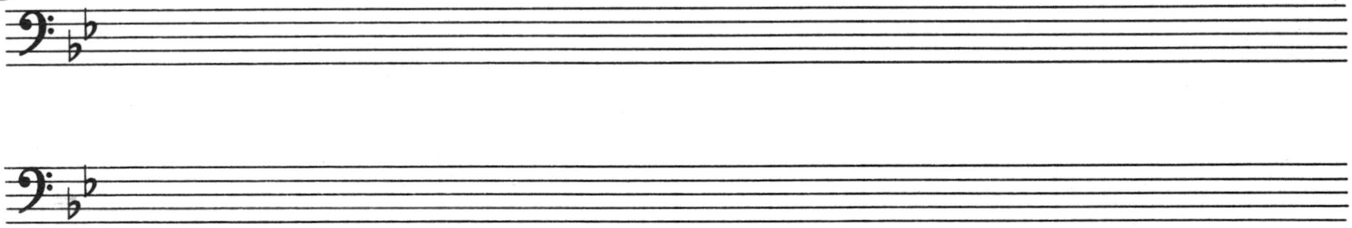

⑤

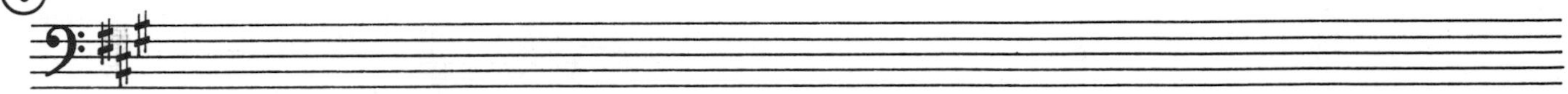

Scoring: 143 86

\- (Px) - (Rx)

_____ (P-score) _____ (R-score)

NEXT INSTRUCTION ON REVERSE

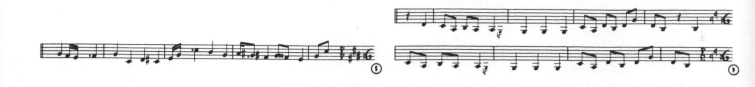

If P-score is 129 or more
AND R-score is 77 or more,
proceed to Lesson C;
otherwise, repeat Lesson B.

Three short melodies are written out below. Each is played once, but with errors, some in pitch and some in rhythm. Follow the music closely and listen for the errors. If you know that there is an error but can't tell what it is, mark x over an incorrect pitch, x under an incorrect beat. If you hear the wrong notes and can identify them, write them into the music. After hearing all three, fold this worksheet up from the bottom to read the answers. Do not score.

A beat, including an upbeat, may contain ♪♪♪ (3)

① (staff with key signature)

(staff with key signature)

② Jot down the notes on the strong beats, which define the measures.

(bass clef staff)

(bass clef staff)

③ (treble clef staff)

(treble clef staff)

④ (treble clef staff)

(treble clef staff)

⑤ (bass clef staff)

(bass clef staff)

Scoring
of Part 2:   143   92

        -      (Px)   -   (Rx)

_____ (P-score)   _____ (R-score)   NEXT INSTRUCTION ON REVERSE

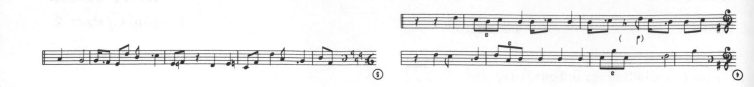

If P-score is 129 or more
AND R-score is 83 or more,
proceed to Lesson D;
otherwise, proceed to CC.

Name:

Date: Instructor:

UNIT FOUR

Lesson CC

(1)

(2)

(3)

(4)

(5)

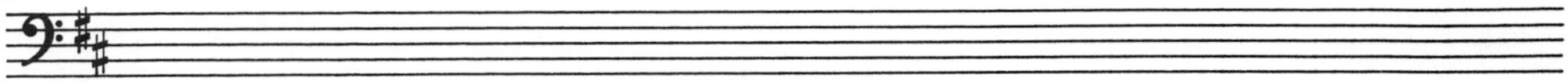

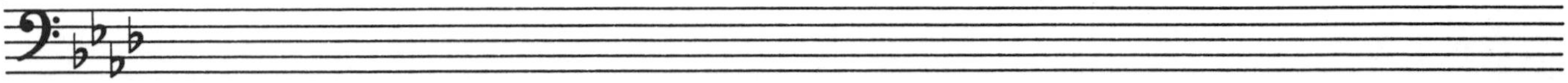

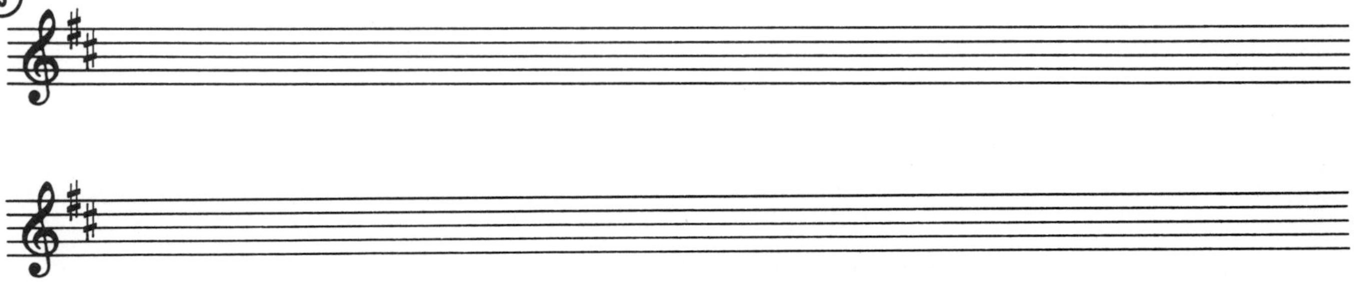

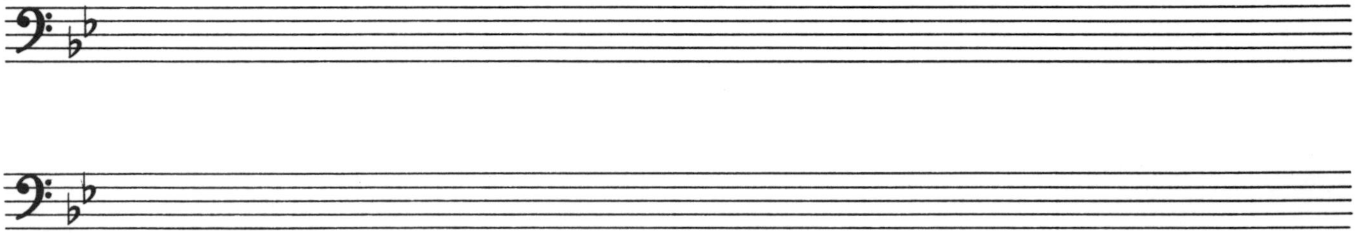

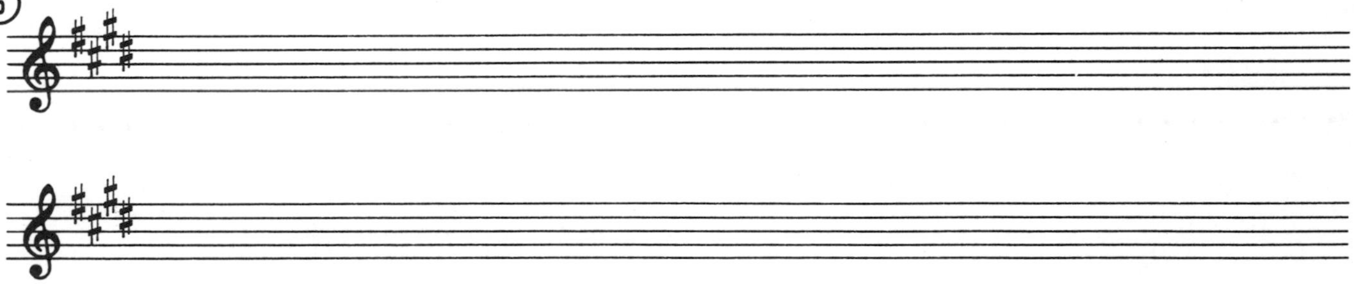

Scoring: 121 83

- (Px) - (Rx)

_____(P-score) _____(R-score)

NEXT INSTRUCTION ON REVERSE

If P-score is 109 or more
AND R-score is　75 or more,
proceed to Lesson D;
otherwise, repeat Lesson C.

Outline these two melodies, selected from Bach cantatas.

①   The first follows a single line of thought.

②   The second implies two lines of development. Indeed, there is the suggestion of a third.

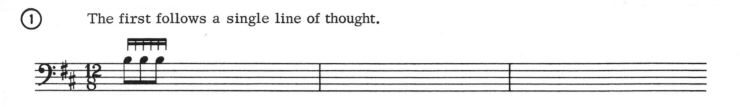

Upbeats may now include ♪♫

①   Listen for the triadic outline in this melody by Pergolesi.

②

③

④   Grace notes are included in this melody from Brahms's Second Symphony. Write them in your answer, but do not score them if incorrect.

⑤   This melody, on which Brahms based a set of variations, has an unusual phrase structure.

Scoring
of Part 2:   133   86

      -       (Px)   -   (Rx)

      _____ (P-score)   _____ (R-score)   NEXT INSTRUCTION ON REVERSE

If P-score is 120 or more
AND R-score is 77 or more,
proceed to Lesson E;
otherwise, proceed to DD.

Name:

Date: Instructor:

UNIT FOUR

Lesson DD

(1)

(2) Outlining will help.

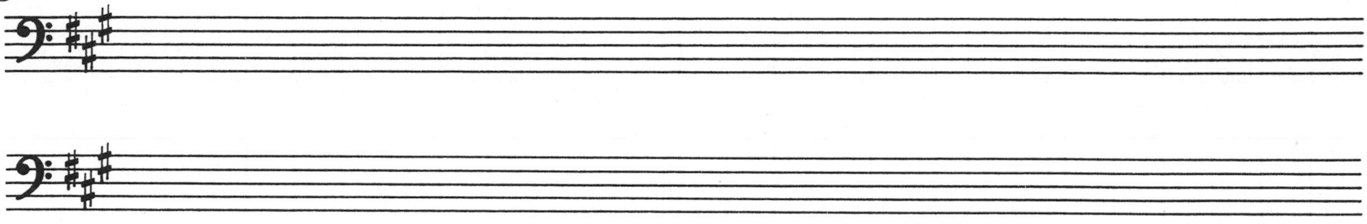

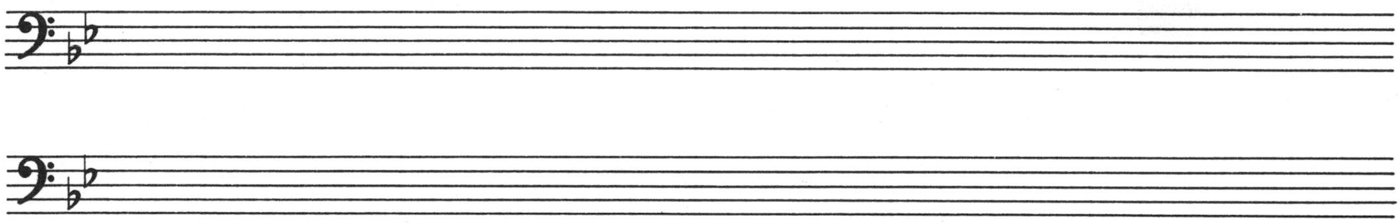

(3)

(4) The two phrases of this melody by Mozart are similar, but not identical.

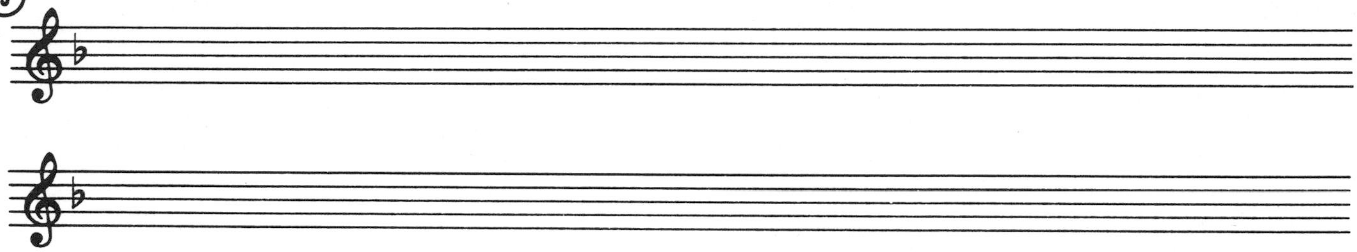

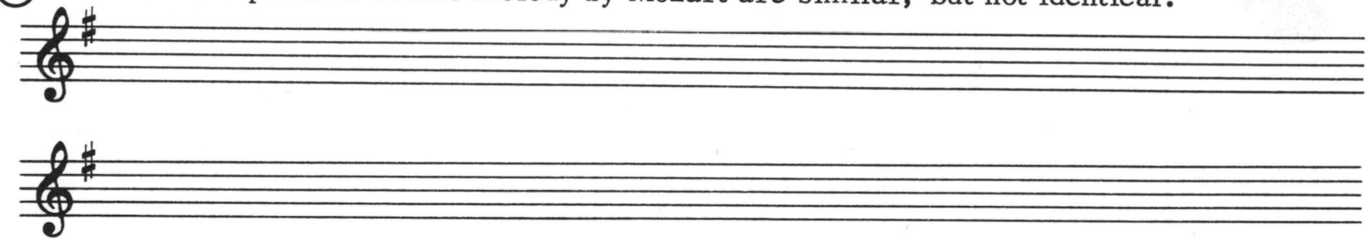

(5)

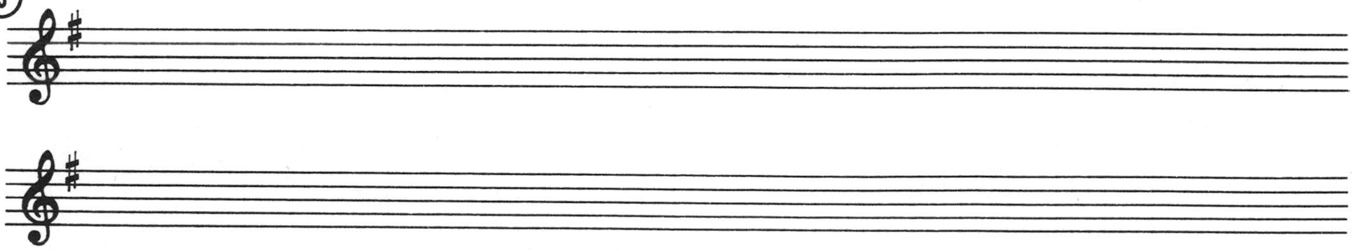

Scoring: 141 80

- (Px) - (Rx)

____ (P-score) ____ (R-score)

NEXT INSTRUCTION ON REVERSE

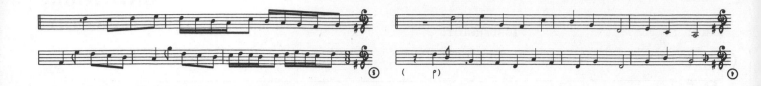

If P-score is 127 or more
AND R-score is 72 or more,
proceed to Lesson E;
otherwise, repeat Lesson D.

Three short melodies will be played once each. Memorize, sing back, and write down quickly. After completing all three, tear this worksheet up from the bottom, and fold so that you can read the answers to Part 1. Do not score.

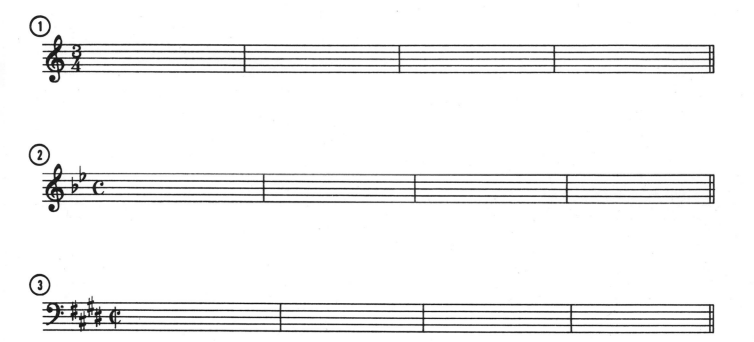

When ♩ is the unit, an upbeat may consist only of ♪

① The first melody consists of two **very similar phrases,** both of which begin with the same upbeat.

②

③

④ Listen for the goal at the mid-point of this tune.

⑤

Scoring
of Part 2:   134   71

        -      (Px)   -   (Rx)

        _____ (P-score)   _____ (R-score)   NEXT INSTRUCTION ON REVERSE

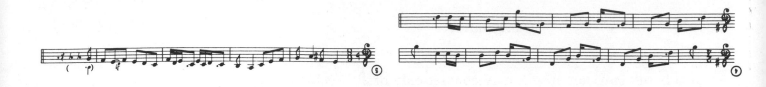

If P-score is 121 or more
AND R-score is 64 or more,
proceed to Lesson F;
otherwise, proceed to EE.

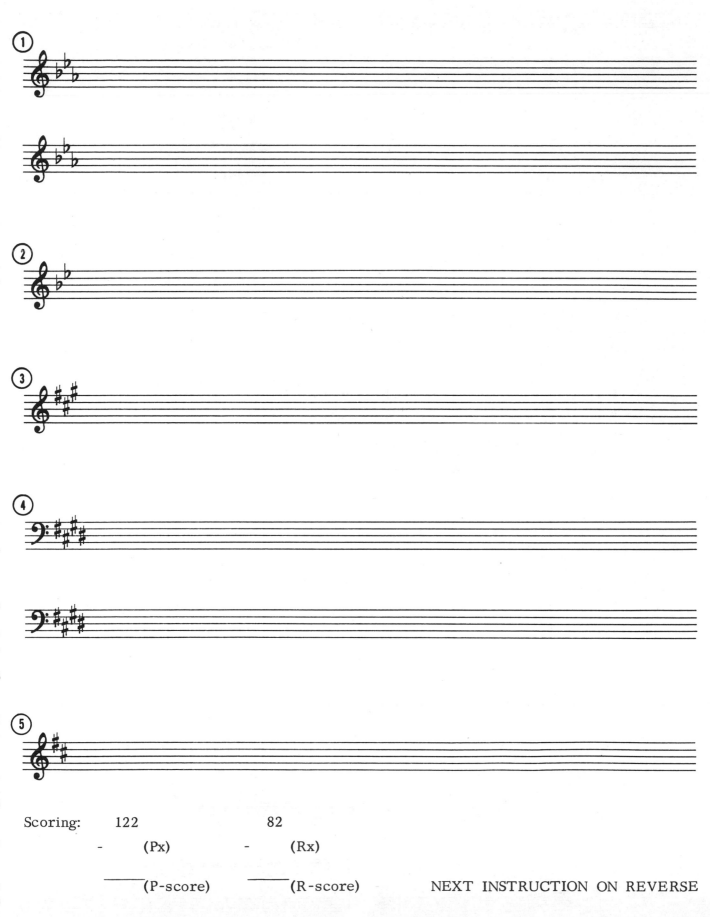

If P-score is 110 or more
AND R-score is 74 or more,
proceed to Lesson F;
otherwise, repeat Lesson E.

Three melodies are written below. Each is played once, but with errors in pitch and in rhythm. Follow the music closely and listen for the errors. If you know that there is an error but can't tell what it is, mark x over an incorrect pitch, x under an incorrect beat. If you hear the wrong notes and can identify them, write them into the music. After hearing all three, fold this worksheet up from the bottom to read the answers. Do not score.

Name:

Date: Instructor:

UNIT FOUR

Lesson F/Part 2

When ♩. is the unit, an upbeat may consist only of ♪

(1)

(2)

(3)

(4)

(5)

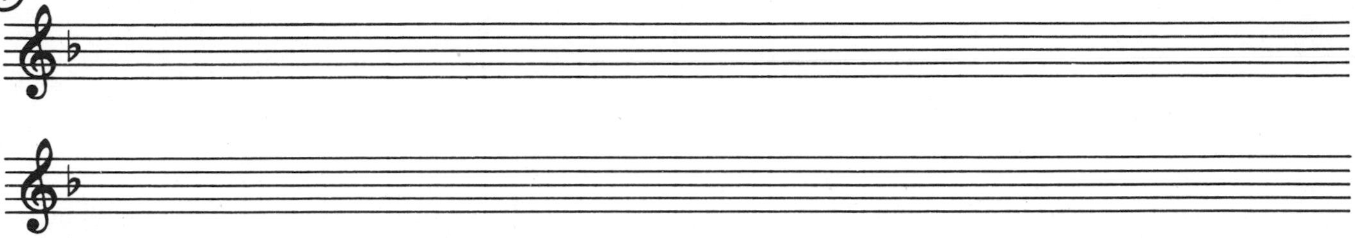

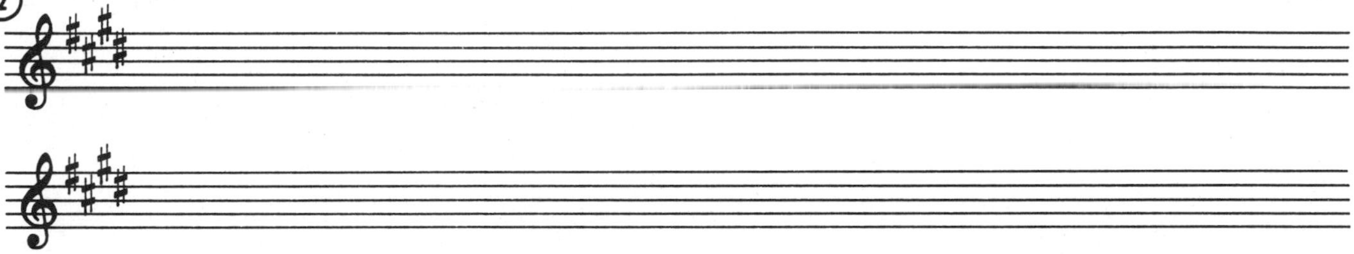

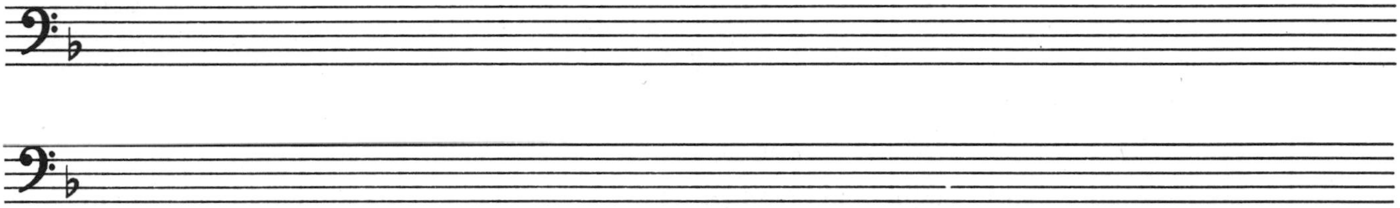

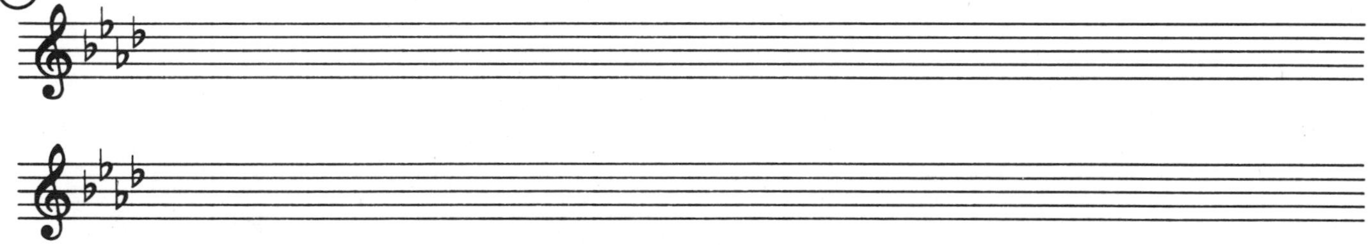

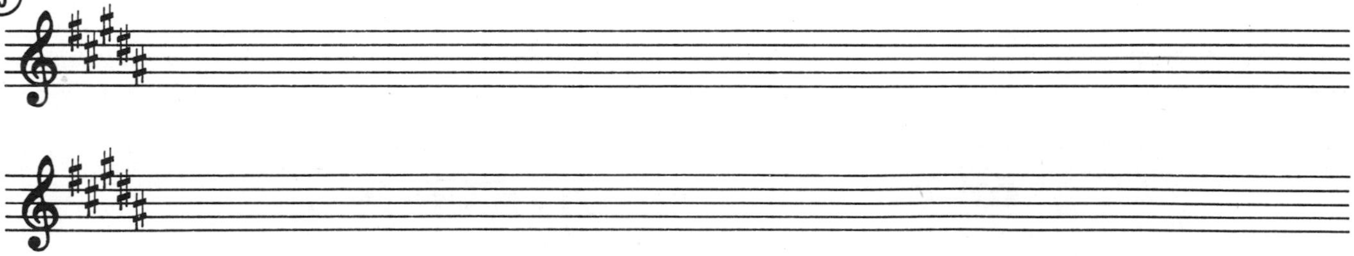

Scoring
of Part 2: 174 108

\- (Px) - (Rx)

______(P-score) ______(R-score)

NEXT INSTRUCTION ON REVERSE

If P-score is 157 or more
AND R-score is 97 or more,
proceed to Lesson G;
otherwise, proceed to FF.

Name:

Date: Instructor:

①

②

③

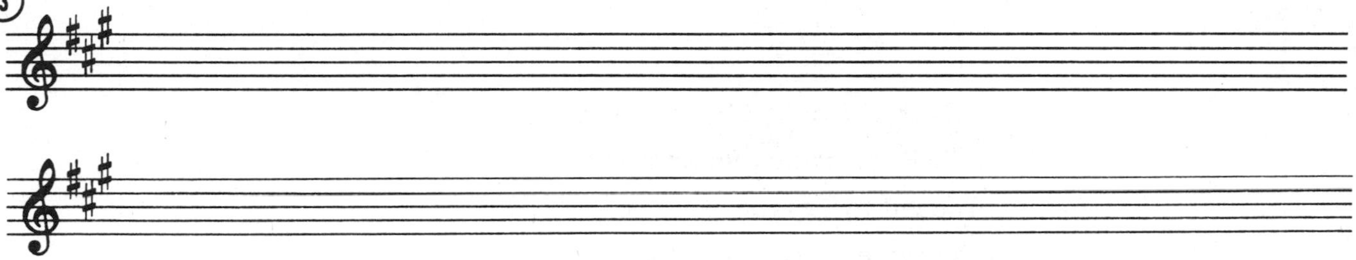

④

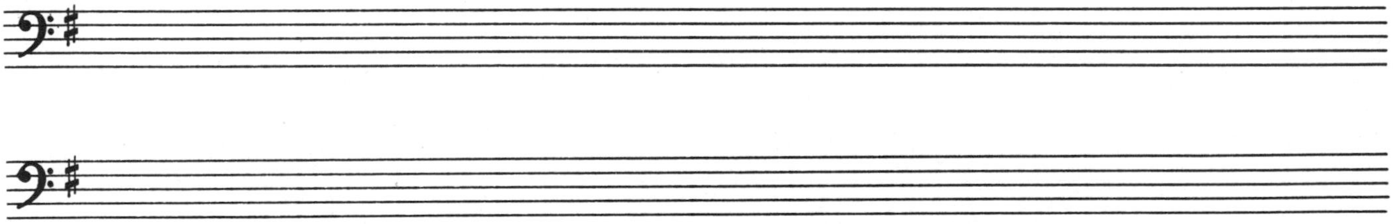

⑤

Scoring: 166   107

        -      (Px)   -   (Rx)

_____ (P-score)   _____ (R-score)   NEXT INSTRUCTION ON REVERSE

If P-score is 149 or more
AND R-score is   96 or more,
proceed to Lesson G;
otherwise, repeat Lesson F.

This is a summary Lesson, with only one part. There are no cues.

Scoring: 155   81
                    -        (Px)   -   (Rx)

                _____ (P-score)   _____ (R-score)   NEXT INSTRUCTION ON REVERSE

If P-score is 139 or more

AND R-score is 73 or more,

you have completed Unit Four;

otherwise, proceed to GG.

A Practice Lesson is available after G or GG.

Name:

Date: Instructor:

This is a summary Lesson. There are no cues.

① (treble clef, 3 sharps — staff)

(treble clef, 3 sharps — staff)

② (treble clef, 1 sharp — staff)

③ (bass clef, 3 flats — staff)

(bass clef, 3 flats — staff)

④ (treble clef, 4 flats — staff)

(treble clef, 4 flats — staff)

⑤ (treble clef, 4 flats — staff)

(treble clef, 4 flats — staff)

Scoring: 140   81

          -       (Px)   -   (Rx)

_____ (P-score)   _____ (R-score)   NEXT INSTRUCTION ON REVERSE

If P-score is 126 or more
AND R-score is 73 or more,
you have completed Unit Four;
otherwise, repeat Lesson G.
A Practice Lesson is available after GG.

The same procedure is followed as in the double-letter Lessons. Each melody, preceded by the preliminary note (tonic), is played three times.

Scoring: 239

-          (total x)

_____ (score)   CONVERSION TO LETTER GRADES ON REVERSE

Conversion to letter grades:

A: 239-216
B: 215-192
C: 191-168
D: 167-144

Name:

Date: Instructor:

The same procedure is followed as in the double-letter Lessons. Each melody, preceded by the preliminary note (tonic), is played three times.

①

②

③

④

⑤

Scoring: 210

             -        (total x)

             _____(score)   CONVERSION TO LETTER GRADES ON REVERSE

Conversion to letter grades:

A: 210-190

B: 189-169

C: 168-148

D: 147-127

The same procedure is followed as in the double-letter Lessons and the Review. Each melody, preceded by the preliminary note (tonic), is played three times.

①

②

③

④

⑤

Scoring: 241

            -          (total x)

         _____ (score)

SOURCES OF THE MELODIES

UNIT ONE

Lesson F   1. Brahms, Symphony No. 2: 1st mvt.

UNIT TWO

Lesson D   4. Mozart, *Eine kleine Nachtmusik*: 1st mvt.
            6. Brahms, *Variations on a Theme of Haydn*: coda
            7. Schubert, *An die Freude* (song)

Lesson E   3. Mozart, Violin Concerto, K. 218: 1st mvt.
            7. French folk song, *Savez-vous planter les choux?*

Lesson F   5. Bizet, *Carmen*

UNIT THREE

Lesson A   3. Bizet, *Carmen*
             4. Haydn, Quartet, Op. 3, No. 3: 3rd mvt.

Lesson AA   3. Brahms, Violin Concerto: 1st mvt.
             5. Haydn, Symphony No. 104: 4th mvt.

Lesson B   1. Beethoven, Violin Concerto: 1st mvt.
             5. Mozart, Quartet, K. 589: 1st mvt.

Lesson BB   1. Haydn, Quartet, Op. 20, No. 4: 1st mvt.
             4. Beethoven, Piano Sonata, Op. 79: 3rd mvt.

Lesson C   2. Bach, Passacaglia in C minor
             3. Mozart, Piano Concerto, K. 488: 1st mvt.
             4. Wagner, *Der fliegende Holländer*

Lesson CC   2. Purcell, Harpsichord Suite in D major
             4. Vivaldi, Concerto for Strings in F major

Lesson D   1. Brahms, Symphony No. 1: 4th mvt.
             2. Bellini, *Norma*
             3. Mendelssohn, Symphony No. 4: 2nd mvt.
             4. Smetana, *The Bartered Bride*

Lesson DD   5. Beethoven, Symphony No. 6: 3rd mvt.

Lesson E   3. Pergolesi (?), Concertino for Strings in G
             5. Haydn, Quartet, Op. 53, No. 3: 4th mvt.

Lesson EE   1. Haydn, Quartet, Op. 20, No. 1: 1st mvt.
             3. Schubert, German Dance
             5. Haydn, *The Creation*

Lesson F   1. German folk song, *Wie komm' ich denn zur Tür herein?*
             5. Handel, Concerto Grosso, Op. 6, No. 10: 4th mvt.

Lesson FF	2. Verdi, *Il Trovatore*
	4. Beethoven, *Rondo a capriccio*, Op. 129
	5. Haydn, Quartet, Op. 76, No. 3: 3rd mvt.
Lesson G	3. Brahms, *Sonntag*
	5. Beethoven, Quartet, Op. 18, No. 1: 1st mvt.
Lesson GG	1. Schubert, Symphony No. 5: 3rd mvt.
	3. Keiser, *Croesus*
	5. Haydn, Symphony No. 92: 1st mvt.
Practice Lesson	1. Ragué, Symphony, Op. 10, No. 1: 1st mvt.
	4. Haydn, Quartet, Op. 3, No. 5: 3rd mvt.
Review	1. Mendelssohn, *Song Without Words*, Op. 53, No. 5
	2. Mozart, Piano Concerto, K. 595: 1st mvt.
	3. Rossini, *Il Barbiere di Siviglia*: Overture
	5. Schubert, *Moment musical*, No. 6

UNIT FOUR

Lesson A	1. Haydn, Symphony No. 101: 3rd mvt.
	3. Beethoven, Violin Sonata, Op. 12, No. 3: 3rd mvt.
	4. Mozart, Symphony, K. 183: 4th mvt.
	5. Haydn, Cello Concerto in D major: 3rd mvt.
Lesson AA	1. Donizetti, *L'Elisir d'amore*
	3. Haydn, Symphony No. 104: 3rd mvt.
	4. Beethoven, Trio, Op. 70, No. 2: 3rd mvt.
Lesson B/Part 1	1. Mozart, Minuet, K. 2
	2. Verdi, *Il Trovatore*
Part 2	1. Haydn, Symphony No. 100: 3rd mvt.
	3. Haydn, Symphony No. 94: 3rd mvt.
	4. Ragué, Symphony, Op. 10, No. 1: 3rd mvt.
	5. Haydn, Quartet, Op. 20, No. 5: 3rd mvt.
Lesson C/Part 1	1. Mozart, *Le Nozze di Figaro*
Part 2	4. Verdi, *Aida*
Lesson CC	1. Thomas, *Mignon*
	5. Haydn, Quartet, Op. 33, No. 6: 3rd mvt.
Lesson D/Part 2	1. Pergolesi, *La Serva padrona*
	4. Brahms, Symphony No. 2: 3rd mvt.
	5. Brahms, *Variations on a Theme of Haydn*
Lesson DD	4. Mozart, Symphony, K. 200: 4th mvt.
	5. Bach, *The Well-Tempered Clavier*, Book 1, No. 15
Lesson E/Part 1	1. Brahms, Quartet, Op. 51, No. 2: 3rd mvt.
	2. Mozart, Sonata for Piano Four Hands, K. 358: 1st mvt.
	3. Brahms, Symphony No. 4: 1st mvt.
Part 2	1. Beethoven, Bagatelle, Op. 33, No. 6
	2. Smetana, *The Bartered Bride*
	4. Thomas, *Mignon*
	5. Brahms, Clarinet Quintet: 1st mvt.

Lesson EE	1. Haydn, Quartet, Op. 33, No. 2: 3rd mvt. (Trio)
	2. Vivaldi, Concerto for Strings in B♭ major: 1st mvt.
	4. Beethoven, Trio, Op. 11: 2nd mvt.
	5. Keiser, *Croesus*
Lesson F/Part 1	3. Mozart, *Die Zauberflöte*
Part 2	1. Mozart, Quartet, K. 421: 4th mvt.
	3. Donizetti, *L'Elisir d'amore*
	5. Brahms, Clarinet Quintet: 4th mvt.
Lesson FF	1. Bellini, *Norma*
	2. Haydn, Quartet, Op. 76, No. 5: 1st mvt.
	3. Mozart, *Le Nozze di Figaro*
	4. Bellini, *I Puritani*
Lesson G	2. Beethoven, Quartet, Op. 18, No. 4: 1st mvt.
	3. Mozart, Quartet, K. 421: 3rd mvt.
	4. Beethoven, Quartet, Op. 18, No. 4: 2nd mvt.
	5. Brahms, Clarinet Quintet: 4th mvt.
Lesson GG	4. Haydn, Quartet, Op. 20, No. 5: 1st mvt.
Practice Lesson	1. Donizetti, *L'Elisir d'amore*
	3. Weber, *Der Freischütz*
Review	2. Schubert, Quartet in D minor: 1st mvt.